JAMES SMETHAM
and
FRANCIS DANBY

Two 19th Century Romantic Painters

London
ERIC & JOAN STEVENS
1974

First published 1974 by Eric & Joan Stevens,
74 Fortune Green Road, London NW6 1DS

Francis Danby in Bristol 1814-24

© Edward Malins, 1974

**Some Reflections on the Career of James Smetham,
with a catalogue of his pictures**

© Morchard Bishop 1974

ISBN 0 9502351 13

Printed in Great Britain by Lowe and Brydone (Printers) Ltd.

Acknowledgements

For their help, advice and permission to reproduce illustrations we are indebted to The Curator, City Art Gallery, Bristol (plates 1-13), The Stone Gallery, Newcastle-upon-Tyne (plates 14-17 and 19), J.S. Maas & Co. Ltd., London (plates 18 and 21) and Geoffrey Grigson, Esq. (plate 20).

Contents

List of Illustrations

Francis Danby in Bristol 1814-24

By Edward Malins

Francis Danby was born on 16 November 1793, the twin son by a second marriage of James Danby, a squireen of County Wexford. Before he was five, his father narrowly escaped assassination at the hands of the rebels in the '98 Rebellion. Despite Wolfe Tone's hopes for United Irishmen, bloody fights had broken out in Wexford between Catholics and Protestants, the insurrection being led by Bagenal Harvey of Bargy Castle, a close relation of James Danby's first wife. Therefore he moved with his family to the comparative safety of Dublin, but died there in 1807[1]; his Will, proved in that year, like all others, being burnt in the destruction of the Four Courts in the Civil War, 1922. Francis's mother was left to bring up three children with little money, so doubtless, was not pleased when her son showed ability in drawing, the arts not being a lucrative profession. However, she put him in the drawing schools of the Royal Dublin Society, where he must have been talented, for in 1812 he held his first exhibition, from which Archdeacon Hill of Dublin bought his picture, 'An Evening Landscape', for fifteen guineas.

Two of his friends in the Dublin classes were George Petrie (1789-1866), afterwards the distinguished map-maker (Ordnance Survey of Ireland), antiquarian, watercolourist, illustrator ('Guide to the Lakes of Killarney') and President of the Royal Hibernian Academy; and James O'Connor (1792-1841), the landscape painter whose pupil Danby is said to have been. But as he was only a year older than Danby, never such an able draughtsman, and the pupil of the somewhat prosaic William Sadler, it is unlikely he taught Danby much. Petrie's father was a successful Scottish miniature painter and engraver settled in Dublin, who had made a drawing of Robert Emmet during his trial in 1803. In early

[1] W.G. Strickland, *A Dictionary of Irish Artists* (1913) vol. 1. p.252.

[1]

June 1813, Petrie, O'Connor and Danby set out for London, primarily to see the Royal Academy Exhibition and to meet other artists. Petrie was the leader, who took with him an introduction to the P.R.A., Benjamin West.

W. Stokes, *Life of George Petrie* (1869), relates how the three visited the R.A. in June and were particularly excited by Turner's 'Frosty Morning', which was **the** picture of the year. Just as Samuel Palmer never forgot Turner's 'Orange Merchantman', seen in similar circumstances in 1819, so 'Frosty Morning' was fixed in Danby's memory. The painting was a magical evocation of a moment at dawn on a cold, misty, October morning in bleak Yorkshire fields, the rising sun silhouetting field workers and cart horses; in the distance, an approaching stage coach with light on, and the ground covered in white, thawing hoar-frost; inspired, so Turner tells us, by James Thomson's *The Seasons*, 'Autumn', (lines 1168-71):

> And now the mounting sun dispels the fog;
> The rigid hoar-frost melts before his beam;
> And, hung on every spray, on every blade
> Of grass, the myriad dew-drops twinkle round.

Thomson 'paints pictures' in his verse by close contemplation of Nature, with an artist's eye, and like Wordsworth later, can conjure up a scene with words which often become the primary inspiration of painters like Danby who also closely observe that same Nature.

In July 1813, after a short visit to Wales where they sketched, Petrie and O'Connor became short of money, so Petrie decided to return forthwith to Dublin (first generously giving the others two gold rings for them to sell), and then O'Connor and Danby walked to Bristol from London in order to take the boat to Ireland. On arrival they had not sufficient money for official lodgings, but stayed above a bakery in Redcliffe Street, then a somewhat disreputable area of the city. The next day they walked to a more respectable quarter and found, at 43. College Green, what is described in the contemporary *Mathew's Directory* as: 'Mintorn, John, Ornamental Pasteboard manufacturer, Stationer and Print Seller', and, in a few years time, also as 'Reading Room and Circulating Library'. John Mintorn, junior, who sketched and subsequently became a life-long friend of Danby's, in a letter published at the time of Danby's death,[1] relates how he met the two

[1] *Western Daily Press*, 20th Feb. 1861.

artists in 1813, bought two of Danby's drawings of the Wicklow Mountains, 'slightly coloured on letter paper' for eight shillings (nothing apparently of O'Connor's), then for the next few days took them out on sketching parties to the Avon Gorge, the Downs above Clifton, and Leigh Woods on the other side of the river. The wooded beauty of the steep Gorge immediately suprised and delighted them, as it had many others. According to Joseph Farington (*Diary*, 27 Feb. 1808), Henry Fuseli had declared it was 'the finest scenery in the kingdom — sublime etc.' And Robert Southey described St. Vincent's Rocks in the Gorge as 'rich with fantastic foliage, the sublime and the beautiful by the boat-load'. For a drawing which admirably depicts the spirit of the Gorge, see the magnificent watercolour by Thomas Girtin, reproduced in Martin Hardie, *Water-colour Painting in Britain*, vol. 2. illustration 12. As a result of the sketching parties on which he had been taken, Danby decided to remain in Bristol. On the other hand, James O'Connor took the boat to Dublin, from where he continued to make repeated visits to England and the Continent, yet did his best work in Ireland: 'View of the Salmon Leap at Leixlip' (c.1818), 'The Eagle's Rock, Killarney' (c.1820) and 'View on the Dargle' (R.A. 1822) are typical of his Irish work — romantic, picturesque, freely painted, and drawn with figures set in wooded scenes through which there is a play of light on a grand scale. See 'The Devil's Glen.' (Plate 13).

Danby was so struck by Bristol scenes and by the stimulus of seeing paintings in England, that he told a friend, who wrote of him in *The Art Journal, 1855*, that 'They increased my ambition, and from my twentieth year I have been an English artist.' Within a short time of his arrival in Bristol he was patronized by a Mr. Joyce Fry, a rich baker and his landlord, who had a house nearby in Somerset. It was there that Danby met his future wife, Hannah, who according to John Mintorn, was 'a very pretty lass, and our friend very naturally fell in love.' By 1818 they had four sons.

This raw youth, with little education or reading, gradually found himself the chief landscape artist in Bristol — there was no other of any skill — and he slowly got to know literary men and artists of all ages who showed him drawings and paintings, or discussed literature or lent him books from their libraries, and took him on their sketching parties in the surrounding countryside. His portrait by his friend John King (1788-1847), now in the City Art Gallery, Bristol shows his fair hair, strong clear-cut features and somewhat nonchalant air, as he holds his brush to paint. He had an independence, bred from solitude, was shy

[3]

and reserved, so found social contacts not superficially easy; but he was amiable and likeable, though stubborn, and certainly made life-long friendships from his Bristol period. Among this group which included him, was the Reverend John Eagles (1784-1855), a Bristol-born scholar, poet and amateur artist, who wrote in 'Blackwood's Magazine' under the *nom de plume* of 'The Sketcher', and also in 'The Gentleman's Magazine'. He was a lovable man, and a verbose writer, but many of his sketches of trees and water show a lively vigour in a Gaspar Poussin manner. As an art connoisseur who knew many artistic and literary people in Bristol, he was of much help to Danby, until 1822 when he left Bristol to take a living at Halberton in Devon. 'A painter cannot too much study poetry' he said, and this is a clue to much of Danby's subsequent work. Many of this cultured Bristol group had been friends of Coleridge, Southey and De Quincey when they were in Bristol some few years previously, and among these was John King (a surgeon who lived in Clifton, not to be confused with John King, the painter). Another friend of Danby's was George Cumberland, senior, then in his sixties, the friend of William Blake, and a man who was especially happy in the company of young people who delighted in his radical ideas, his freshness and humour. His many interests in addition to the Fine Arts show in the subject-matter of some of his letters to the local newspapers throughout his life: the education of the poor, the state of Bristol gaol; the installation of gas lighting; propulsion of vessels by a jet of water, and the teaching of the blind by embossed letters.

Like Cotman earlier, Danby's technique in watercolours required time, with planned construction and detailed drawing on a flat table later. As recommended in Varley's *Treatise on the Principles of Landscape Design*, which came out when Danby was in Bristol, the arrangement of light and shade is carefully planned, and much attention is given to objects reflected in water, at which Danby is incredibly skilful. The locale of nearly all of the drawings is either the Avon Gorge, or a charming romantic glen of the river Frome at Stapleton, within walking distance of Danby's Bristol house. Usually, his washes are clean and orderly, though in some of the later drawings there is blotting and scraping out which tends to obscure the brilliance. His honest observation of weeds and wild flowers used in his foregrounds, and of reflections in water are distinctive, but notable above all is his depiction of figures set in the landscape, often catching a low evening sunlight.

The earliest dated drawing[1] is a 'View from near Shirehampton'

1820, 5⅜ x 7⅞, which is signed and dated on the stern of a barge in the lower right of the picture. It is a naturalistic drawing with minute figures on the bank breaking stone, and, of no great interest. Of about the same date is 'A view of St Vincent's Rocks: the Avon Gorge', 17¾" x 26¾", a large watercolour, again signed on the stern of a boat. Its definition is by tone rather than line, in the manner of Girtin and early Turner. In its wildness it heralds Danby's later apocalyptic oil painting. 'The Avon at Clifton', 5" x 8⅜", is a superb little drawing, looking across the river to Clifton on a still evening with a magical sky lighting the shadows on the water. Danby uses a strong and deep colouring for this romantic landscape with its solitary figure on the bank. 'The Frome at Stapleton' 5¾" x 8½", in its solid execution and body colour seems to indicate his turning to oil·painting. These drawings and others are all in the City Art Gallery, Bristol.

There are many English watercolourists at this time whose work is not dissimilar to Danby's and is equally capable. But there are no painters in oils whose work is like his. The seven small paintings, c. 1820-23, in the Bristol Art Gallery are sufficient to prove this. All of these are in excellent condition and show his best work during his decade in Bristol. (1) 'A View of the Avon Gorge', panel, 13"x 18", looking down the river on a calm summer's evening, shows a small family group seated under trees on the grass in the foreground, the father in a beaver hat and brown tail coat pointing out to his little daughter the details of a wherry sailing towards them; other small figures, whose faces catch the low sun, walk or talk. Danby's colours here are rather dry, but he has a good impasto in the high-keyed parts. The tree overhanging the group has delicately painted leaves and trunk similar to William Blake's treatment. (2) 'The Snuff Mill, Stapleton', board 8¾ x 12, has lovely painting of a bank of distant trees against a cobalt sky, rather like Elsheimer in feeling; three children in the foreground, one lying on his stomach on a stone breakwater by a weir, in a red coat, white trousers and country hat, reminding one of Constable's treatment of country boys. (3) Another larger picture of the Snuff Mill, canvas, 15¼ x 24¼, painted from the lower side of the building where trees overhung the Frome from a steep bank; water

---

[1] I am grateful to Eric Adams, *Francis Danby*, unpublished Ph.D. thesis, 1969, London University for this and certain other information about the pictures. Adams' definitive work, *Francis Danby*. (Yale) was not published when this article was written.

[5]

falling over a weir, and dark, moist undergrowth in the foreground; in the distance at the back of the Snuff Mill, a brilliant blue sky and bright cumulus clouds, through a gap in the trees through which Turneresque shafts of light pierce; a boy fishes in the dark foreground. Once again, Danby's reflections in the water are most magical. (4) 'A Boy fishing at Stapleton', board, 5 x 7¼, is filled with striking, luminous green textures, and the boy is dramatically highlighted by a low shaft of sunlight through the trees; in the middle distance, other children play in a field in which cattle are grazing; one small girl in brilliant blue dress of neo-classical design. An astonishing wealth of detail in so tiny a picture. (5) 'A Scene in Leigh Woods', panel, 13 x 19¾. An oldish man, neatly dressed in a frock coat and high hat, is being read to by a young girl in a white dress as they rest in the late afternoon on the neat grass of a glade, surrounded by trees on a rocky bank which rises to the skyline. Other more distant figures, one a child, appear to be walking or enjoying the scene, which does not, however, bear much resemblance to any part of Leigh woods, and the drawing has been shown in the Arts Council exhibition, 'The Romantic Movement' 1959, entitled 'Blaise Castle Woods'. The composition is original and unclassical, with a tree trunk half in the picture on the right, and a road which runs out of the picture in the foreground. The relationship of Man to Nature in this and to some extent in all these pictures reflects the influence of Coleridge in its intimacy and suitability — no submerging of Man by Nature's sublime forces in dark, and melancholic scenes, but a bright clarity and appropriateness in the relationship, which is reflected in the somewhat tight handling of the brush-work. Nature has been tamed but not spoilt by Man. (6) 'Clifton Rocks from Rownham Fields', panel, 15¾ x 20, is the largest of these paintings. Once again the Avon Gorge is seen in the afternoon light, with sailing wherries and barges; a bright blue, clear, sky contrasts with the ochre sandstone rock and soil, which is the predominant tone of the painting. In the foreground, a group of children, resting, is highlighted by the sun under a huge oak tree whose branches and leaves, delicately painted, cover the whole of the top of the painting, but are parted sufficiently to show the tower of the Observatory on the other side of the river. In the foreground Danby has painted, in much detail, ragwort, nettles, ferns and other wild flowers, almost in a Caspar Friedrich manner, but with none of his sinister hothouse qualities. (7) 'Boys sailing a little boat', panel, 9¾ x 13¼, has a most romantic use of sunlight, but with no sky, striking through trees on to a group of children, all of whom except one, who is engaged in

[6]

sailing his little model boat, are standing on a bridge of planks looking down into the water. The treatment of the concentration of the children, engaged in their absorbing play, and the careful painting of the play of light and shadow, common to all of this group of paintings, are most noticeable, and this has obviously been enhanced by the recent cleaning of this picture.

One of the commonest features of the Bristol paintings by Danby is the depiction of children beside water and stream, dreaming, fishing, playing or resting. His attitude to childhood activities is inherent in these scenes: a happiness in the children's absorption in their activity which he nearly always highlights to draw attention to it. This acceptance of the beauty of children at play must have come from William Blake through George Cumberland, for nothing was further from the general attitude of the time. The 'Moral Songs' of Isaac Watts expresses the common view of childhood — that work in the affairs of the world was virtue alone. But for Blake, virtue in childhood was in the land of the imagination where they might dream. 'What eternally exists, really and unchangeably'; that was reality in the imagination.

> Father. O Father! what do we here
> In this land of unbelief and fear?
> The land of Dreams is better far,
> Above the light of the Morning Star.

Compare those lines of Blake's with Watts' Sluggard (in his 'Moral Songs'. No.1) who will not work and who wishes for

> A little more Sleep, and a little more Slumber,
> Thus he wastes half his Days, and his Hours without Number.

Like Blake's thousands of little chimney-sweepers who are released in their dreams by an Angel, Danby's children are placed in a landscape of Virgil's Elysium:

> Then down a green plain leaping, laughing they run,
> And wash in a river, and shine in the sun.

Around them Danby paints wild flowers and weeds with loving care, with none of the sinister detail of Caspar Friedrich and the German school; the Meadow Rue, Campion, Vetch, Ragwort and Willow Herb growing by the banks of the Avon or Frome, not appearing exotic as from an overheated studio. The freedom expresses a joy which is absent

[7]

from Watts' conception of a garden as untidy when not tended by the Sluggard:

> I past by his Garden, and saw the wild Bryar,
> The Thorn and the Thistle grow broader and higher;

Danby's children come from poorer classes but are never in rags; and they differ from those painted by Mulready who are nearly always caught in some act for which adults are showing disapproval, or are competing with or apeing adults unnaturally, rather than being just children. Some of Danby's children may be poor, yet there is none of the timid anxiety of Watts' children, and no pity shown for them; but a delight in their play in these natural settings, nearly always illuminated by shafts of sunlight through the trees.

At the same time as Danby was painting in this genre he was endeavouring to make an impression of the R.A. and the British Institution by paintings of suitable size. These took two forms: the first is really only an enlargement to exhibition size of the type of painting we have been discussing. One of the first, 'Disappointed Love' (1821) 24¾ x 32, now in the Victoria and Albert Museum, was shown in the R.A. of that year. A young girl, in a brilliant white dress, is seated on the banks of a stream, (like the river Frome), her head, bowed in dejection, resting on her raised knees over which her long dark hair falls. The pose is identical to the figure for Blake's added plate for *America* (1793) illustrating 'As when a dream of Thiralatha flies the midnight hour'. Torn pieces of a letter float away from her down the stream; beside her an open locket, her red cloak, ribboned straw hat and small shoes — all epitomizing her innocence. The figure is in strong light, but today the stream and the overhanging boughs of the trees are almost totally blackened. Evidently the surface pigment has become transparent so that the dark underpainting appears through it. But the colour range must always have been restricted to these dark tones except for the girl and her garments. Near her are the fern-like drooping leaves of pasque flowers like those of William Blake's title page to *The Book of Thel,* and also, symbolically, a rose briar with thorns, similar to Blake's 'The Sick Rose' from *Songs of Experience.* The foliage on the bank is like that in the larger painting of the Snuff Mill, Stapleton; but the picture as a whole is far from being in its state of preservation. It created a furore at the R.A. and was eventually bought by the great collector, John Sheepshanks.

[8]

In 1821 the best picture of the year at the B.I. was thought to be John Martin's 'Belshazzar's Feast'; the huge architectural scale, black clouds, rocks, frantic figures, and apocalyptic manner being a great popular sensation. Martin had been painting these doom-laden canvases for some years, and Danby evidently thought he could get in on this band-wagon. This was Danby's second method of gaining the notice of the wider public in the metropolis, and so he suddenly plunged into the maelstrom of apocalyptic painting in the John Martin manner, with a vast canvas entitled 'The Upas, or Poison Tree of Java', 66 x 90, which was shown at the British Institution in 1819. Like the young Holbein in his painting, 'The Ambassadors' (National Gallery), with its puzzling symbolism of the anamorphosis of the perspectively distorted human skull in the foreground, Danby meant to surprise viewers and engage patrons. According to Redgrave, the upas tree was in a moonlight glen (The Valley of Death) in the midst of skeletons on the ground, one living man covering his face with his hands, and a vulture falling dead. It was obviously a horror tale in the Gothic novel tradition of Mary Shelley's *Frankenstein* (1818); 'a grand scene of desolate rocks by moonlight' wrote George Cumberland, senior. An upas tree had been described by Erasmus Darwin in an appendix to his extraordinary poem, 'The Loves of the Plants' (1789); its poison being so strong that it killed everything for ten miles round, and a human being, if pierced by a poisoned dart within a few minutes. (The whole affair was a complete myth). Danby, like Coleridge, must have read Erasmus Darwin's poem and he may have seen J.M. Gandy's 'Pandemonium or part of the High Capital of Satan' (R.A. 1805) and been influenced by Turner's *Liber Studiorum*, Plate LXIII, the engraving where Rispah is sitting on the ground amidst skeletons and corpses. Anyway, Danby's 'Upas' was the shock piece it was intended to be, though it is now impossible to judge as a painting,[1] for such were the brown bituminous paints used by Danby that is is almost invisible, and indeed, it had darkened badly by 1854.[2] But in this genre it cannot be compared with Martin's 'The Fall of Babylon' in the same exhibition at the B.I., or with his 'Belshazzar's Feast'. However, Danby made a name for himself in this genre and Martin's subsequent 'Deluge' was considered by Thomas Lovell Beddoes (whom Danby would have met in Clifton) to be 'rascally plagiarism upon Danby'.[3] Another similar painting of

1. Now at the Victoria and Albert Museum but stored in Ham House, Mdlx.
2. G.F. Waagen, *Works of Art and Artists in England*, London, 1838.
3. Letter to Barry Proctor. March 1826.

Danby's 'The Delivery of Israel out of Egypt' (1825) was quickly sold to his first noble patron, Lord Stafford, for five hundred guineas. In that year Danby was made A.R.A.

By then he had moved permanently to London, having been sending work to exhibitions from a London address since 1824, not completely losing touch with Bristol as he lived near George Cumberland jnr. in Mornington Crescent. All seemed set for a brilliant career when Sir Thomas Lawrence bought his 'The Raft: Sunset at Sea after a Storm' R.A. 1824 (not now known to exist), which was startling in its extravagant tones: a thousand hues of vermilion and purple reflected in the sea between bold and lavish clouds. A half-naked figure on the raft told the obvious story. But despite the P.R.A.'s support, all was not as well with Danby as it appeared. He had left Bristol without telling any of his friends where he was going, and his oldest supporter, George Cumberland, wrote in May 1824 to his son:

'Danby is a good artist, but very opinionated, and is I fear a ruined man. He has a wife and children and pupils, but I believe through total thoughtlessness is over head and ears in debt; he has left this place hastily and secretely.'[1]

He must have needed little persuasion from Sir Thomas Lawrence to move permanently to London, where opportunities for artists, both in seeing paintings and in obtaining patrons were so much greater. But the exact moment he chose to leave was unfortunate, for it coincided with the foundation of the 'Bristol Institution for the Advancement of Science, Literature and the Arts', which included a Philosophic and Literary Society, all housed in elegant rooms in Park Street, where there was a lecture theatre, museum, Exhibition Hall and reading room with scholarly journals. Bristol, compared with other provincial cities like Dublin, Exeter, Newcastle and Liverpool, was slow to encourage the arts, its citizens being interested, then as now, in politics and commerce. The original members of this Society included a cross-section of the local gentry, the professions, and merchants such as Henry Wills (tobacconist) and Richard Fry (chocolate maker), as well as honorary members whose names give some indication of the scope of the Society: Sir Humphry Davy, Michael Faraday, Sir Thomas Lawrence, Robert Southey and James Watt. Danby's friend, John King, who painted historical scenes and portraits, said in a lecture to the Society in 1825:

1. British Museum. MS 36510.

'The love of Art has I trust more than dawned at Bristol. The praiseworthy of exertions of the Directors of its Institution to bring fine works of art before the public appear to be more and more appreciated .'[1]

After Danby had left Bristol for London permanently, the Reverend John Eagles anonymously published a lament for his departure, which he attributed to Bristol's lack of support for the arts. It also reveals Eagles' ideas of painting, and his own literary background, from which Danby must have benefited when he knew him prior to his departure from Bristol for Devon. The poem, written in Latin, but with a convenient translation, was published by Felix Farley of Bristol on 1st May, 1826, and entitled *Rhymes by Themaninthemoon:*

> Ye painters, people wood, and lawn
> With fairy, satyr, nymph and faun;
> Not vulgar bumkins, coarse ill-bred,
> All sweating for their daily bread;
> At ancient Grecian fables glance,
> Of Ariosto's sweet romance
> Of rescued dame and broken lance,
> Of shelter'd loves in hollow nooks,
> By which shall run enchanted brooks.
> — Embody from the sacred page,
> Stories of patriarchal age —
> — Or theme sublime — the fiery rain,
> Departing hot, the blazing plain;
> Heaven's vengeance upon Egypt dealt;
> It's blood, — it's darkness to be felt;
> These, these are the themes, that may proclaim,
> So Danby finds, an artist's fame.
> Learn this ye painters of dead stumps,
> Old barges, and canals, and pumps,
> Paint something fit to see, no view
> Near Brentford, Islington, or Kew.
> Paint anything — but what you do.
> Did Bristol give no fostering care
> To efforts such as Danby's; where,
> Where are his pictures, on whose walls?
> Not I, neglected genius calls.

---

1. *Minutes. Philosophic and Literary Society. May 1827.* MS. City Archivist's Office, Bristol.

These lines contain exact references to Danby's pictures: the 'ancient Grecian fable' of Calypso grieving for her lost lover in 'An Enchanted Island', 1824; 'Ariosto's sweet romance' or 'Orlando Furioso' which Eagles was translating when he died, in 'Landscape with Warriors of Old Times' showing armed men, 1823; 'Shelter'd loves in hollow nooks' in 'Disappointed Love', 1821; 'Heaven's vengeance on Egypt' in 'The Delivery of Israel out of Egypt', 1827. Conversely, Eagles' dislikes: 'vulgar bumkins, coarse, ill-bred' in the genre scenes of the Dutch school; 'old barges and canals' of Constable; and the 'view near Brentford, Islington or Kew' presumably of many lesser topographical artists.

George Cumberland regretted that Themaninthemoon had ceased his writing in Felix Farley's newspaper, so wrote to him on 13 March 1829:

> 'There was a time when you gave us weekly, charming flashes of poetic light from the Man in the Moon . . . but lately you are all for political and polemic war; for my part I haunt still the woods and charming dells that surround us where Bird, Eagles and Danby . . . and Jackson, with other artists and amateurs innumerable once peopled them in peaceful harmony and tranquil enjoyment of the enchanting scenes of Leigh.'[1]

Had this artistic dawn arrived earlier in Bristol it would have helped Danby himself to obtain patrons, now his pupils gained. In June 1824 and April 1825 the Institution held exhibitions of Old Masters from West Country collections, which were seen by thousands. The high standard may not be appreciated without reference to the exhibits; but, for example, the Collection of Philip John Miles, M.P. of Leigh Court, contained the Altieri Claudes now in the National Gallery, Titian's 'Venus and Adonis'; a Rubens 'Holy Family', and 'The Conversion of St. Paul, Raphael and Rembrandt portraits etc. Young local artists were given free tickets to the exhibition at the Institution. The Minutes of the Committee State:

> '26th June 1824. 'Resolved that a ticket for admission be given to Mr. Poole (a young artist)[2] son of Mr. Poole, Coal Merchant.'

For a 'Modern Masters Exhibition' (post-1700), Danby's painting, 'Solitude; the Moment of Sunrise, The Moon rising over a Deserted City' was obtained from London and 'placed on an easel' for the last

1. George Cumberland, *Occasional Correspondence*. MS. Bristol Reference Library.
2. John Falconer Poole, R.A. 1861, who later played an unfortunate part in Danby's domestic life.

two weeks of the show. George Cumberland jnr did a watercolour sketch of this painting with its cold green shadows and golden light. It fetched only 5½ guineas in the sale room in 1912, being in a poor state, and has since disappeared.

In 1829 a domestic scandal occurred which became public gossip and totally ruined Danby's career. No one knows exactly what it was; but the Royal Academy reacted sharply, and he was never made an R.A. as it was felt he had disgraced the profession of artist. The next year he became self-exiled for eleven years, leaving the country with his mistress, Helen Evans, and his seven children, first to Paris and afterwards to Geneva, then retiring to Exmouth for the rest of his life. His marriage had broken up and Hannah Danby seems to have gone off with the young Bristol artist Paul Falconer Poole, (see above) who also went into a sort of 'exile' in Southampton for some years. She married him directly after Danby's death in 1861. Richard and Samuel Redgrave, *A Century of Painters* (1866) write that 'an unhappy marriage shivered his household gods'; F.M. Redgrave, *Richard Redgrave, a Memoir* (1891), 'a scandal the Academicians could not condone'; and Richard Garnett, *A Dictionary of National Biography:* 'some insurmountable domestic difficulty overtook him'. But *The Art Journal* (1861) in its obituary notice of Danby is critical of the R.A. Committee:

> 'The Academy will never get rid of the charge of having upon evidence not altogether tenable, repudiated one of the greatest painters of the age and country, and a man possessed of many endearing qualities.'

Thus did his early marriage, which he later described to Richard Griffin as 'unadvised and unknown to my friends', result in 'a precarious and unhappy life'.[1] Despite this, the decade in Bristol provided him with the opportunity to meet a group of literary and artistic friends whose influence was felt throughout his life, and certainly enabled him to produce work in Bristol which was some of the best that he ever did. The eclecticism which started him painting in the apocalyptic style of John Martin was disastrous, for his work was never as good as Martin's, perhaps because Martin was a religious man and therefore believed in the Old Testament incidents which he painted. Divine retribution lived for him, but not for Danby, who should be known for the smaller Bristol landscapes, in which humanity

1. Richard Griffin, *Rank and Talent of the Time* (1861)

finds a place in a kindly Nature which is uniquely seen by Danby in all its detail of water, trees and lawn. I should like gratefully to acknowledge help and expert advice freely given by Francis Greenacre, Curator of the City Art Gallery, Bristol, who collected the best examples of Danby's work for the exhibition of Bristol artists, September to November 1973. It helped to raise Danby's reputation, which is slowly recovering from almost total neglect for eighty years after his death.

Some Reflections
on the Career of James Smetham

By Morchard Bishop

(i)

'The work of James Smetham who went out of his mind in middle age is almost unknown, but a self-portrait reproduced in his published *Letters,* and other still-existent works prove that he had talent, while the letters themselves suggest that he had genius. Ruskin encouraged him and classed him 'among my best friends', Rossetti never doubted that he had an unacknowledged genius. His letters are full of intelligent comments, such as this: "Don't get into the focus of Criticism. Many men spoil their enjoyment of Art by looking on it as something to pull in pieces, rather than something to enjoy and lead them to enjoy nature, and through nature to enjoy God. How wretched is that feverish, satiated, complaining spirit of criticism. Never contented, never at rest. 'Is this better than that, these than those? Is this a great man, and if great, *how* great?' . . . all the while avoiding *The Thing* and its relish: not thinking art, but about art; not conversing with nature, but with names." '

That was John Piper[1], writing in 1942. And here is Dante Gabriel Rossetti, a good many years earlier, in the 1880 edition of Gilchrist's *Life of Blake:* '[James Smetham], a painter and designer of our own day who is, in many signal respects, very closely akin to Blake; more so, probably, than any other living artist could be said to be. James Smetham's work — generally of small or moderate size — ranges from Gospel subjects, of the subtlest imaginative and mental insight, and sometimes of the grandest colouring, through Old Testament compositions and through poetic and pastoral themes of every kind, to a special imaginative form of landscape. In all these he partakes greatly of Blake's immediate spirit, being also often nearly allied by landscape

1. *British Romantic Artists* pp. 35-36.

[15]

intensity to Samuel Palmer, — in youth, the noble disciple of Blake. Mr. Smetham's works are very numerous, and, as other exclusive things have come to be, will some day be known in a wide circle. Space is altogether wanting to make more than this passing mention here of them and of their producer, who shares, in a remarkable manner, Blake's mental beauties and his formative shortcomings, and possesses besides an individual invention which often claims equality with the great exceptional master himself.'

Not then, assuredly, a negligible man, this Smetham; but he has been dead — or as good as — for the better part of a century and his tracks are no longer easy to follow. What comes hereafter, then, must largely be of an exploratory nature, written in the hope that it may do something towards bringing again to light further examples of those 'very numerous' works of Smetham to which Rossetti refers, that now it is to be feared languish in unvalued — perhaps unrecognized — obscurity.

(ii)

Central to any rediscovery of Smetham must come, I think, certain events that took place in 1854. On almost the last day of the October of that year, F.D. Maurice's Working Man's College opened its doors at No. 31, Red Lion Square, and among Maurice's more impressive captures in the way of staff for it had been Ruskin, who had volunteered to supervise a drawing-class. Within a week of the founding of the College no fewer than a hundred and thirty enthusiastic students had enrolled themselves as members, and one of them had evidently been James Smetham, since, as early as the conclusion of Ruskin's first — or possibly his second — session, Smetham had produced for the great man's inspection a selection of his drawing-books. That was on November 10, and Ruskin had taken the books home with him to look them over at his leisure. The result of his investigations was the following letter which, no doubt, must have quite overwhelmed Smetham, coming as it did from the revered author of *Modern Painters*:—

Denmark Hill, 15th Nov. 1854.
My dear Sir,

I am quite amazed, almost awed, by the amount of talent and industry and thoughtfulness shown in these books of yours. What is the nature of your artistic occupation? I am very anxious to know all that you are willing to tell me about yourself. Please let me keep the

[16]

volumes at least till Tuesday next. I cannot look them over properly sooner; and meantime send me a line, if I may ask you to take this trouble, telling me what your real employment in life has been, and how your genius has been employed or *un*employed in it.

Faithfully yours, and obliged,
J. RUSKIN.

To this, immediately on receipt apparently, Smetham despatched the following colossal reply:—

16th Nov. 1854.

Dear Sir,

It is kind of you to show such an amount of interest in my scribblings, and to express so much sympathy in my pursuits. I fear you overrate the work, and that my desires and your approbation will not be justified by anything worthy of permanent regard.

I have, however, a great love for art and all that concerns it, and have devoted my life to its pursuit; nor can I resist the opportunity of informing you what has been the course of my history: not so much because I look on it as at all remarkable, but because you are, I am persuaded, capable of understanding without a long explanation why I should find pleasure in telling it at all.

Beginning at the beginning, I must inform you that I am the son of a Methodist preacher, who spent his life in periods of two or three years in various towns of the kingdom with only one object in view. My first awakening to consciousness, as far as I can remember, was in a valley in Yorkshire, outside the garden gate of my father's house, when at the age of two years. I have a distinct remembrance of the ecstasy with which I regarded the distant blueness of the hills[1] and saw the laurels shake in the wind, and felt it lift my hair. Then I remember thinking my elder brother one of the cleverest lads alive, because he drew a horse and a bull-dog in water-colours; and also at four years of age running away on the nearest heath — that was at Nantwich, in Cheshire — and delighting in the little pools, which were called pits. At eight I recall a moonlit night, when the moonlight had the effect of enchantment on me, and I listened softly to the noises of the night. I took to drawing about the same age with a box of water-colours which ought to have cost fourpence, but which, by my frequent asking the price, the good woman let me have for threepence. That was at Congleton, in Cheshire. From that time I formed the desire and design of becoming a painter,

1. *cf.* 'A child painter will find it a bliss to notice that the distant hills are of a fine Titianesque blue long before he knows what Titian was or has seen a picture.' *Lit. Wks.* p. 108

and afterwards never had a thought of being anything else, and made my father promise to let me be one. At eleven, from Leek, in Staffordshire, I went to a boarding-school at Woodhouse Grove, in Yorkshire, where the sons of Methodist preachers are educated, or ought to be; and where I ought to have learned more than I did. There I copied Raphael's cartoons from the *Penny Magazine*[1]. What time was not consumed in drawing was spent in prowling about the Grove and slipping away to Calverley Wood, and inventing ghost-stories to fit old Calverley Hall. On leaving school I was articled for five years to E.J. Willson, of Lincoln, a Gothic-architect, who wrote the literary part of Pugin's *Examples of Gothic Architecture.* His office was at the Castle, in a round tower; and there I ought to have learned more architecture than I did, but I was always drawing Comuses and Satans and Manfreds. Mr. Willson was very fond of painting, and very kind. He scolded me before my face, and praised me to my fellow-clerk behind my back; and at length, to effect a compromise, set me to draw all the figures about the Minster. I spent a grand solitary year at this work. With a key to myself I poked about every corner at all hours, and twice a day heard the organ-music and the choristers' singing roll about among the arches. I sat on the warm leads of the roof, and looked over the fens, and dreamed and mused hours away there, and then came down over the arches of the choir and drew the angels drumming and fiddling in the spandrils. I made a large and careful drawing of the Last Judgement from the south porch, and had a scaffold up to it to measure it. But I fretted my soul because I wanted to be a painter, and at length boldly asked Mr. Willson to cancel my indentures, who said decidedly that he would not, and that De Wint, the painter, who was coming down shortly, would put that and other foolish notions out of my head; for painting was precarious, and few excelled in it or could live by it. This he meant, I doubt not, in great kindness. When De Wint came, he said he could sympathise with me, having been in similar circumstances himself, and advised Mr. Willson to let me go, which he did at the end of three years, my father's approbation having been previously secured by myself. I was thus thrown on the world by my own act and deed, and with very little practice announced myself in Shropshire as a portrait-painter, getting employment at once; working when I wanted money, strolling to Buildwas and Wenlock and Haighmond [Haughmond] Abbeys, and scrambling to the top of the Wrekin, and

1. *Penny Magazine,* Vol. I, p.348 (Dec 1, 1832) and Vol. II, pp.17. 76; 125, 172, 220, 261 (Jan 19 – July 6, 1833).

wandering in lane and meadow and woodland. I went on after this fashion till 1843, when I came to London and entered as a probationer in the Royal Academy, having previously drawn a little while at Cary's. I made no doubt that getting into the Academy I should keep in, and drew, I suppose, carelessly, for at the end of three months I did not get the student's ticket. I went to Jones to see how I ought to have done my work, taking some drawings with me. He told me not to be anxious, for in or out of the Academy I should succeed. I sent in another drawing as probationer, and got in again, intending to look about me more, but was suddenly called away into the country.

I went into the neighbourhood of Bolton Abbey, where my father then resided; and here you will understand me when I speak of the great change which came over my life. The death of my brother (a Wesleyan minister in London) cast a great shade over my wild dreams and extravagant ambitions. I did a great deal for his approbation, and when he had gone my spirit followed him. I perceived that to attain to him was not a matter of fancy or speculation, and 'the commandment' came to me. A complete uproar and chaos of my inward life followed, and I fell into the 'slough of despond'. The beauty of nature mocked me, my fancies become ghosts. I felt my discordances with the spiritual universe; and it was not till my father also died that my soul was stilled and set in order. I had worked on (except for one dreadful period of four months, when I could not work at all, though in perfect health) wearily and painfully; but now I resumed my pursuits with new zest, and devised the plans of study, some of the results of which you have seen. My views of art were changed in some particulars, and I think enlarged, but I dared no longer strive on my old principles and impulses. A salutary fear shut me up in a happy seclusion, and I could not precipitate myself into the battle of life; so I went on painting portraits and interspersing them with fancy pictures, gaining money enough to keep me, and then snatching a month or two for study; now in a large town, now in a little one, now in a remote farm painting the farmer and his family, and roaming in his fields and by the edge of his plantations; then in London.

I exhibited in Liverpool first in 1847[1] ; at the Academy in 1851, -2, -3, and -4, but the last two years my best picture was returned and the portraits put in.

I ought to mention another feature of my life. While studying I

1. The catalogues of the Liverpool Academy make it probable that this date should be 1848.

became so impressed with the importance of form as an universal *language* that I was boring all my friends with its utility, and inveigled young men to tea that I might talk myself hoarse in persuading them to draw everything. But they did not profit, and I longed for some sphere where I could advance the cause of drawing as an element of education, and demonstrate my own theories. My fever was allayed by a request that I would undertake the instruction in drawing of a hundred students, who were in course of training to be teachers, at the Wesleyan Normal School, Westminster. I accepted it; and for three years one of my happiest duties has been the fulfilment of my task of four hours a week there. I teach model and freehand drawing, and perspective. The staff of teachers then became my circle, the objects of the institution part of my life; and I completed the connection six months ago by marrying the teacher of one of the practising schools there, who still retains her position. Our united salaries make us for the present independent of painting as a means of livelihood, and I have five days in the week for picture-making.

This sums up, I believe, all I need care to tell you of my history. Of my purposes, perhaps, I had better say nothing; of my works nothing.

There is a passage in the second volume of *Modern Painters*, p.136, § 12, 'Theoria the Service of Heaven', which I have half chanted to myself in many a lonely lane, and which interprets many thoughts I have had. I love Art, and ardently aspire, not after its reputation (I think), but the realisation of its power on my own soul and on the souls of others.

I don't complain of want of employment, or anything of that sort; for I have found it easy to earn money when I have set about it, but I have felt the dearth of intercourse on the subject of my occupations, and am pleased with this opportunity of writing to you. With artists generally I have not felt much drawn to associate. In my own associations there is on the part of others little true sympathy with my work. I have to spin everything out of myself; and yet I would not at all be understood to complain; scarcely, all things considered, to wish that things were otherwise.

I have made my letter quite long enough already, and will only reiterate my thanks to you for the kind spirit in which your note was written.

I am, dear sir,
sincerely yours,
JAMES SMETHAM.

This is a revealing document and one cannot help wondering what Ruskin made of it. Quite clearly it was the spontaneous outburst of a man who was starving for companionship, for some kind of comprehension of what he was trying to do: 'there is on the part of others little true sympathy with my work'.

There are other notes equally characteristic: 'I love Art, and ardently aspire, not after its reputation (I think), but the realisation of its power on my own soul and on the souls of others.' This, I think, is a passage crucial to the understanding of Smetham; he hadn't it in him to get worked up about his reputation — fame, high prices and all that — and for this reason he felt an imperfect sympathy for most of his fellow-artists with whom, as he primly remarks, 'I have not felt much drawn to associate'. What, on the contrary, he sought was the effect that art had upon his 'soul' and upon 'the souls of others'; and in order to understand what he meant by this one has, I believe, to consider very carefully that period of his life which he describes as following the death of his elder brother, when 'the commandment' came to him. This evidently was a time of supreme crisis, when 'the beauty of nature mocked me, my fancies became ghosts. I felt my discordances with the spiritual universe'; a time when, 'for one dreadful period of four months', he could do no work. He came through it at last, helped in some strange way by a second death, that of his father, to find his 'views of art were changed in some particulars, and I think enlarged', though he no longer possessed the wish 'to precipitate himself into the battle of life.' As to the nature of this change in his views of Art, I shall have more to say later, but it would seem beyond question that here was the true turning-point of his career, and perhaps the beginning of his period of real mastery. It was also the beginning of that nervous instability which, many years later, was to precipitate him into his ultimate darkness.

Before passing on to these matters, however, there are a number of minor points that need to be made in supplementation of Smetham's own account of his career before 1854. He had been born at Pateley Bridge, a small town to the north-west of Harrogate in Yorkshire, on September 9, 1821, his father being then minister in that parish. As for his schooling at Woodhouse Grove, it is all too evident from the account of that school given by his friend and school-fellow, Dr. Benjamin Gregory, that it was a hideous place, conducted with the greatest ferocity with which was blended an unctuous religiosity of the worst kind. Smetham was a deeply religious man in his distinctively evangelical fashion, but there can be little doubt but that the seeds of many of his future troubles were first fostered by the perfervid atmosphere of this school where, according to Dr. Gregory, on the occasion of the Quarterly Love Feast, 'the sacred flame burst out in the dormitories' and almost every boy 'professed to have found peace with God'. What, in short, was one of the prime causes of Smetham's unease was the belief, similar to that which had afflicted Bunyan, that he was a great sinner and was perhaps numbered among the damned:

> 'Fear tells my heart that I may be
> Some day an alien from Thy door'

he wrote, as late as 1868, in a short poem called 'The Single Wish'. And though he could not have believed this all the time, for his love of nature and his early years of wandering staved it off, it was in his bones, it returned intermittently, so that his breakdown after the death of his brother was almost certainly caused by it, as was his final collapse.

As for his three years in Willson's office, it is only necessary to note in passing the extraordinary parallel between the time spent by the young William Blake in drawing the tombs in Westminster Abbey for his master, Basire, and the way in which the young Smetham was similarly let loose to meditate among the glories of the Angel Choir at Lincoln. To point the parallel, there is a fine passage in Smetham's essay on Blake (*Lit. Wks.* pp.118-9) which enlarges on 'the dreadful beauty, the high majesty, of Gothic shrines and their clinging soul of imagination'.

It is now no longer possible to trace with any precision Smetham's wandering years between the time he left Willson's office and his arrival in London in 1843. Certainly he was painting; 'at eighteen I essayed portraits', he tells us, 'and from that time have maintained myself by painting'. But as well as his tour of Shropshire he must have visited Redditch and Madeley, for at the former place he took up once again with his old school friend, Dr. Gregory, with whom he tramped the Worcestershire and Warwickshire lanes. His conversation at this time (Dr. Gregory tells us) was 'stimulative, recreative, and restful. He loved not to argue, but to expatiate'. What he expatiated on, among other things, were the poems of Tennyson, whose two new volumes of 1842 he had recently acquired.

After the Academy fiasco, Smetham resumed his itinerant way of life, residing for a time in such places as Warrington, Selby, Manchester and Liverpool, and supporting himself by his art. In his essay on Reynolds (*Lit. Wks.* p.20) there is a passage very relevant to the sort of life that he must have been leading as a travelling limner: 'Till about the year 1855 there was no mode of livelihood more secure and pleasant than that of the unambitious country portrait painter of any ability or conduct. Oil pictures of the heads of households were things as necessary to equipment as the sideboard or the sofa . . . Nothing placed two men, who had dealings with each other in those days, on a more pleasant footing than that of painter and sitter.' Alas! Daguerre's invention put an end to all this pleasantness and, as we have seen, Smetham threw up the sponge some four years before the 1855 date which he gives as terminating the business.

He first exhibited, as far as one can tell, at the Liverpool Academy at Old Post-Office Place, Church Street, Liverpool, in 1848, his address at that time being Spring Gardens, Warrington; and thereafter, as he remarks in his letter, at the Royal Academy, from 1851 to 1854.

It was not until 1851 that he obtained his teaching post at the Normal College in Westminister, a post that he retained for twenty-six years; and it was here that he became acquainted with two of his best friends and most frequent correspondents, Professor W.K. Parker and Charles Mansford, the mathematics tutor. William Davies[1], who later wrote the Memoir that prefaces his *Letters*, was an even earlier friend whom he had encountered in Warrington in 1846.

In 1854 he married, settling first in Pimlico, where he was living at the time of his letter to Ruskin. Later, after the birth of his first son,[2] he moved, in 1856, to Stoke Newington, then a comparatively rural neighbourhood. His home there was at 1, Park Lane, Paradise Row (earlier known as Willow Grove), and there he remained until his final breakdown in 1877. Writing some time in 1857, Smetham gives a pleasant picture of his life in Paradise Row:

1. Davies was an interesting man who deserves a note to himself. He was born about 1830 into a legal family long established in Warrington, but was himself something of a dilettante who enjoyed indifferent health and spent a considerable part of his time in Rome. Between 1869 and 1895 he wrote some half-a-dozen books, *The Pilgrimage of the Tiber, from its Mouth to its Source*, (1873) and *A Fine old English Gentleman*, a life of Admiral Lord Collingwood, (1875) being among them. He also contributed to the *Quarterly Review* and *The Architect* (on art subjects) and reviewed books of an Italian ambiance for *The Academy*. Apart from his masterpiece, Smetham's *Letters*, his chief claims now to remembrance are that he tended John Gibson, the sculptor of the tinted Venus, during his last illness (1866) and was the sole fellow-countryman to attend his funeral, and that, during a serious bout of pneumonia in Rome in 1892, be became a patient of the celebrated Dr. Axel Munthe. He died in Chester May 9, 1897. His obituary in the *Warrington Examiner* records that he 'never lost a friend or made an enemy'.

2. His family eventually consisted of four sons and two daughters.

'Our front windows overlook that Paradise, and our back ones overlook gardens, now blossoming. All is peaceful. I have a true studio now all to myself, a sanctum in my home for the first time. I have begun to enjoy it. I walk in the fields and on breezy roads. I am growing familiar with trees and banks and blossoms and clouds. God has given me my heart's desire, and I only desire that I may dwell in Him as peacefully as I dwell in my home.'

It was a happiness that was to be of no long continuance. In the autumn of 1857 he had a second breakdown, and rather strangely it was perhaps his revered Ruskin who had precipitated it. In this way: one of Smetham's drawings bore the title 'The Women of the Crucifixion', and as he had at length decided to do an oil version of this, he had told Ruskin of his intention, at the same time sending the original drawing to him, presumably as a gift. He must, therefore, have been not a little disturbed to receive in reply a letter to the following effect:

Dear Mr. Smetham,

I hardly know whether I am more gratified by your kindly feeling or more sorry that you should think it is in any wise necessary to express it in so costly a way; for costly this drawing has been to you, both of time, thought, and physical toil. I have hardly ever seen any work of the kind so far carried as the drawing in the principal face. I shall indeed value it highly; but if indeed you think any words or thoughts of mine have been ever true to you, *pray* consider these likely to be the truest, that it is unsafe for you, with your peculiar temperament, to set yourself subjects of this pathetic and exciting kind for some time to come. Your health is not sturdy: you are not satisfied with what you do; and have to do *some* work that is irksome and tedious to you. If your work is divided between that which is tedious and that which tries your feelings and intellect to the utmost, no nervous system can stand it; and you should, I am very strongly persuaded, devote yourself to drawing and painting pretty and pleasant faces and things, involving little thought or pathos, until, your skill being perfectly developed, you find yourself able to touch the higher chords without effort. I should like to know, if you have leisure any day to tell me, your entire meaning in this drawing. Is it merely the women at the cross with the multitude behind deriding; or have you intended any typical character in it? . . .

Believe me,

gratefully yours,
J.RUSKIN

[24]

This is a highly significant letter because it shows clearly how soon after making Smetham's acquaintance Ruskin had perceived the fundamental instability that lay at the root of his being. 'Is it merely the women at the cross . . . or have you intended any typical character in it?' Was it, in fact, a symbolical prefiguration of Smetham's own distraction and despair?

Be that as it may, there seems little doubt but that this letter marks yet another change in the direction of Smetham's course and an end to the brief period of ecstatic discipleship that he had enjoyed with Ruskin. The suggestion that he should paint only pretty faces and pleasant things! Evidently Ruskin's Kate Greenawayism was always latent in him, even if, in this particular case, he was, or said that he was, chiefly concerned about Smetham's 'nervous system'. At all events, it is perhaps to the point that when William Davies, in writing his Memoir, came to a discussion of the reasons for Smetham's failure as an artist he laid the blame squarely upon three factors: on Photography, on Pre-Raphaelitism — and on Ruskinism.

(iii)

It is time now, while Smetham is recovering from his 1857 breakdown, to turn to some consideration of the extraordinary régime which for the last dozen years or so — ever since the death of his brother — he had imposed upon himself; for now, at last, this period was closing. So far as it can be understood, this régime seems to have been founded on the belief that the sole purpose of human life was spiritual growth, that the soul was born into the world only in order that it might be expanded and perfected to the Divine standard. (Something, in fact, that much resembled Keats's idea of this world as a 'vale of Soul-making'.) To this end all the mechanisms of his existence were now arranged, all his attention was directed. Even his art became to him a means solely towards the attainment of this purpose; and to further it the most laborious and detailed plans were laid, appalling in their intricacy. Great numbers of pocket-books and notebooks were filled with pictures which illustrated his reading, his thought, his relations with the outer world, his spiritual conflicts and aspirations. Whatever he did, wherever he went, all was recorded; no happening, however trivial, was permitted to be lost or wasted.

To this system of 'putting everything outside of you', as he called it, by recording it in words or drawings, he gave the name of Monumentalism: 'instead of letting ideas die I build to each a lasting monument,' he wrote; adding, in another place: 'What Bewick's tail-pieces are to engraving so is Monumentalism to Painting — Tennyson's Brook compared with the Thames'. The way in which he fashioned these records was by scattering amongst the prose passages of his diary an infinite series of little drawings in pen or pencil which he called Squarings, because each of them was enclosed in a rectangular frame. They were usually very small, not more than 2" by 1", and some of them were beautifully drawn, some mere hieroglyphs.[1] The essence of the matter was that nothing must be lost. The books in which he kept these extraordinary records were called his Knowledge Books, and it is probable that it was some of these which he had shown to Ruskin in 1854. If it were not, then it may well have been some of the other elaborately illustrated volumes that he was simultaneously creating: his four books of Bible drawings done on interleaved sheets, his Shakespeare and his Classical Dictionary similarly treated, his illustrated Wesleyan Hymn Book.

All these last, as well as his Knowledge Books, were amazing productions and are — some of them at least — still in existence. When, some sixteen years or so ago, I had the opportunity of seeing them, my reaction cannot have been very dissimilar to that of Ruskin. Here, I felt, was genius; but what was to be done about it? I showed them to various publishers who all agreed with me that they were very remarkable, but — think of the cost of reproduction and, as well, were they not, let us face it, a trifle eccentric! Smetham had gone mad, hadn't he? and now so many of the clues had been lost, the trails grown cold. No, nothing could be done. Nothing except that, as one fervently hopes may some day be the case, they be lodged for safety in one or other of our public collections. Smetham, in this case as in a good many others, slips through our fingers; we recognise the genius but feel uncomfortably that it is not in the least of the saleable kind.

One further aspect of this regimen of his lasted even longer than the period of the Knowledge Books, and that was his creation of what he dubbed Ventilators. He had always been a prolific letter-writer, though his correspondents were few and for the most part obscure. Now, however, after 'the commandment' had come to him, he found that the normal processes of letter-writing were altogether inadequate to cope with his Monumentalism, his doctrine that nothing must be lost, and so he bethought himself of another device. He made numerous little

1. He has recorded 'the happy hour' when he made his first Squaring: 'It was on February 18, 1848 at 11 p.m. .... it introduced me to a new life.'

paper-books consisting of several sheets of note-paper, each sheet cut horizontally into three slips and the slips sewn together, and these he kept in considerable numbers in his pocket-book, so that, whenever a thought that he deemed worthy of preservation came to him, he was able at once to jot it down, as he walked the streets, waited at railway-stations, sat by his own fireside. In due course, as each little book became full, it was posted to a selected recipient. Originally known as Idea-ventilators, the title of these miniature books was later shortened to Ventilators. Much of that very curious and valuable volume of his so-called *Letters,* which was published after his death by William Davies and his widow, Sarah, must have originated in these Ventilators, which is one of the reasons why that book has so unusual and, in a way, so unconvincing an aspect — for many of its entries do not read like letters.

'This system (says Davies) of writing down himself on every occasion became a part of the daily routine, and had the double advantage of fixing the fleeting moment in a substantial and tangible form, as well as that of affording relief to an oppressed and over-burdened mind.' The 'over-burdened mind', after the illness of 1857, shot off suddenly at a tangent. On the October of the year following we find him describing what had happened:

'I look back with love and wonder and pleasure and thankfulness at the long sand-lane (with occasional mire) into which, for the sake, I am sure, of good and right and pure motives, and better results in the end, I diverged some twelve years ago, and in which I sacrificed almost every outward, palpable, present form of comfort or success. (Strange, that just as I emerged from it I should be called to suffer!) [A reference, of course, to his breakdown.] But I am all through it to the last curve. I have done at least one thing which I intended, and, like Prospero, I have broken my wand and buried my books. Henceforth I belong solely to the outward. It is mine, if spared, to do, to put out, to give; no longer specially to receive. Fool as I am, I am as wise as I expected to be. "The glory dies not, and the grief is past." I now, because of the *monumental* way in which I have prosecuted my designs, cannot by natural law lose anything, but must gain by meditation rather. If I know little, I have learnt the bearing of things — have learnt to admire, to appreciate — richly to enjoy. But the most delightful consequence just now to me is that as the whole stream of labour goes to the outward, I begin to see the results of work.'

With this new sense of 'belonging to the outward', he set forth on

[27]

new paths, attempting book-illustration[1], taking up etching under the aegis of William Bell Scott. His etchings were collected under the title of *Studies from a Sketch Book*[2], and some of them secured the guarded approbation of Ruskin, who wrote, nevertheless:

'But pray, on account of the fatigue, don't work so finely, and don't draw so much on your imagination.'

Kate Greenawayism was still in the ascendant.

After the etchings, Smetham's last throw seems to have been a series of ambitious oil-paintings which I shall describe in a little more detail hereafter.[3] Here it is only necessary to say that two of them were submitted to the Academy Exhibition of 1871, and two subsequently. All were rejected. About a couple of years later a private exhibition of these and other works of his was held at his studio, and a number of the pictures were bought by loyal friends and admirers. Rossetti wrote on this occasion, from Kelmscott, to say:

'You know that your work is of the kind that I really enjoy, because you have always an idea at the heart of it; and what I hear from friends about your latter doings makes me sure that they would excite my admiration even more than former ones. Owing to your plans of life, you have remained as yet much more in the background than could possibly have been the case had your works been more widely seen.'

'Owing to your plans of life'; there was the key. Smetham had never planned for success or recognition; and now it was too late. In 1877,

---

1 As far as I know, the first book that Smetham illustrated was Edward B. Tylor's *Anahuac, or Mexico and the Mexicans* (1861). This volume contains three plates in colour based upon models made by native artists and representing, respectively, The Porter and the Baker in Mexico; Indians bringing charcoal etc. to Mexico; and Indians making and baking tortillas. Each plate is signed J. Smetham *del.*; the engraver was W. West.

The only other book that I have found with a Smetham illustration is also dated 1861 and is a child's book, *Snow-bound in Cleeberrie Grange. A Christmas Story*, by G.E. Roberts, published by Joseph Masters. The woodcut frontispiece, "Lilian Crowned by the King", is signed J. Smetham and engraved by the Dalziel brothers; and what is not without interest is that the book is dedicated to John Ruskin. (See *Other Dated Pictures* in list at end, under year 1861, for the original drawing for this frontispiece).

2. These etchings, all designed and etched on steel by Smetham, seem to have totalled twelve and were published by Williams and Lloyd of 29, Moorgate Street at approximately quarterly intervals during 1860 and 1861. The Tate Gallery possesses a set of twelve: No. 1. Forsake not the Law of Thy Mother. $6\frac{1}{2}$" x $4\frac{1}{8}$". No. 2. The Last Sleep. $1\frac{7}{8}$" x $1\frac{1}{8}$". No. 3. The Days of Noah. $5\frac{1}{2}$" x $4\frac{1}{8}$". No. 4. Hugh Miller Watching for his Father's Vessel. 9" x 12". No. 5. Midsummer. 9" x 12". No. 6. Mr. Robert Levett. 12" x 9". No. 7. The Lord of the Sabbath. 9" x 12". No. 8. The resurrection of the Daisy (Illustration to Chaucer). $6\frac{1}{2}$" x $8\frac{1}{4}$". No. 9. The Death of Earl Siward. $8\frac{3}{4}$" x $6\frac{5}{8}$". No. 10. The Moorland Edge. 7" x 9". No. 11. The Dell. 9" x 7". No. 12. The Water-Lily $7\frac{1}{8}$" x 9". Ruskin especially praised the second of the series, *The Last Sleep*; but it was No. 3, *The Days of Noah*, which, by its elaboration, elicited the caution quoted above.

3. See Catalogue at end.

chaos descended upon him once and for all. He lived on until February 5, 1889, part of the time in an institution; and the stone which his friends set upon his grave in Highgate Cemetery bore an inscription from the 17th Psalm, so fitted to his case that one wonders if he had not selected it himself:

I shall be satisfied when I awake with Thy likeness.

(iv)

What remains now for us to say of the man whose career we have followed thus far? There is, first, his earthly envelope, his appearance, what Smetham himself would very likely have called 'the outward man'. By far the best account we have of this is that provided by William Davies who had first encountered him in Lancashire when, at the age of twenty-five, Smetham had been painting the portraits of some of Davies's relatives. This is what he says: 'His appearance in youthful manhood was striking; indeed his personality was always noticeable as specially characteristic. He bore the stamp of an intellectual beauty strangely attractive. His hair grew in a sort of reckless profusion, tending to the leonine in mass and hue, not reddish, but a low-toned chestnut. His face was harmonious and proportionate, the features delicate, the forehead well pronounced, lofty, and expansive; the nose aquiline, not over-prominent; the mouth firm, rather small, delicately cut; the lips ample, inclined to fulness; the chin refined in mould. He always shaved, only reserving the side-growth, as the beard was unusual when he was young, and he was conservative in his personal modes. His figure was tall and rather spare, with a slight tendency towards the student's stoop. He always wore a frock coat, a loose necktie, the bow carelessly tied by his own hand, and invariably clothed throughout in black. There was a sort of wavering or undulating motion in his gait [as was the case also, we are told, with Coleridge], slightly expressed, and sometimes a certain movement with the hands indicated — how may it be described? — as if feeling or groping towards the Unknown, in the endeavour to seize something not wholly out of reach, but still eluding the grasp. This was quite unconscious to himself, doubtless, and not marked, but when observed was significant. The expression of the eye was feminine in softness, but at the same time wide and earnest, laden with the spirit's message. His manner was distinctly reposeful, and had nothing of haste or fidgetiness in it. He was always gentle, kindly, and courteous to all. I never heard him use a harsh tone or saw him assume a commanding manner to any

[29]

one at any time. He was patient and forbearing in all things; reserved in speech on ordinary occasions, never interrupting another, easily overborne in talk, saying nothing often when he felt and thought much. One did not always get at his opinion easily, and it might have been supposed on some occasions he had none, but on waiting inquiringly for it it was given in a decided form, clear, nervous, unmistakeable.

'His conversational powers were remarkable when he was in the vein, but so unforced that unless moved to speech I have known him to remain a whole day almost without uttering a word. When he did speak he never failed to command a hearing. Whether serious or jocular, one was met by a freshness of view and aspect at once arresting' — and Davies then proceeds, at some length, to describe his powers of comic narration.

This description of the outward man is borne out by the self-portraits that still exist. One of them is a small oil of 1844, now in the Ashmolean, to which Smetham has affixed the title, 'Thoughts too deep for tears'. It shows him almost full face, with long flowing hair, a Shelleyan open-necked shirt, and beautiful eyes that express a certain bewilderment, a certain incredulity. He was only twenty-three when he painted it and he was undoubtedly a very handsome young man, who might almost equally have been a very handsome young woman. It is a face that reveals great potentialities both for strength and for weakness — particularly about the mouth; and considered simply as a portrait it is a masterly piece of work.

Another striking though very different portrait is the oil that is reproduced in sepia as the frontispiece to his *Letters*. This was painted in 1853 and remained in the Smetham family until about 1966, when it was sold to Messrs. Agnew. It is a later but fined-down version of the same appealing countenance though the cheeks are less full and the forehead seems higher because the hair has been carefully brushed back. The open shirt has been replaced by a loose collar and a flowing tie; he has a book in his hands and his eyes regard you steadily with an expression of great, though somewhat questioning, intelligence. This, doubtless, is the maturer Smetham who, dressed with that austerity which befits a disciple of Wesley, carried out his tutorial duties at the Normal College in Westminister.

There may also be found, in the most unexpected of places, some further description of Smetham, though it is doubtful how much of it is portraiture and how much caricature. This is in Theodore Watts-Dunton's very queer and indeed frantic novel, *Aylwin,* in which

Smetham figures as the character called Wilderspin. Since Watts-Dunton's chief purpose in this story is to give an account of the Dante Gabriel Rossetti that he knew in earlier years, he does not take any great pains to get Smetham right, and indeed uses him chiefly as a foil to the Rossetti character, D'Arcy. Even so there are some touches that seem authentic: Smetham's austerity of appearance is well hit off, 'That's the first time,' says one of the characters, 'that I ever saw a painter shaven and dressed in a coat like a Quaker's'; indeed, some of the low-life people in the book have a nickname for him — they call him 'the shiny Quaker'. Other aspects of his peculiarities are roughly sketched in: he is a 'rare rum 'un', speaks with a North-country burr, in a voice of striking power and volume, is even said to have 'goggle eyes'. He is variously described as a visionary spiritualist; a religious enthusiast whose genius is very nearly akin to mania; a spiritualist painter, one-third artist, one-third madman and one-third seer. It is also alleged that his 'addled brains are crammed with the wildest and most ignorant superstitions'. What is his creed? someone asks. Is it Swedenborgianism? Of the school of Blake, perhaps? suggests another. 'Of the school of Blake', replies Wilderspin. 'No. He was on the right road; but he was a writer of verses! Art is a jealous mistress . . . the painter who rhymes is lost.[1] . . . I am my own school; the school of the spirit world.' Someone else remarks of him that he's in love with a model, only to get the reply, 'If you think Wilderspin to be in love with any woman, you little know what love is. He is in love with his art.'

There are other Wilderspinian utterances which, perhaps, are partially characteristic. One, made thrice in the book, relates to 'that base Darwinian cosmogony which Carlyle spits at, and the great and good John Ruskin scorns. The age is gross . . .; the age is grovelling. No wonder, then, that Art in our time has nothing but technical excellence; that it despises conscience, despises aspiration, despises soul, despises even idea — that it is worthless, all worthless.' In another place he dilates upon scepticism, 'the curse of the age,' he calls it. 'There is nothing real but the spiritual world.'

Among Wilderspin's more expansive *obiter dicta* which ring relatively true are these: 'No one who has never wanted food knows what life is [one recalls at once Gissing's ever-reiterated question regarding his fellow-artists: 'Has he starved?'] . No one has been entirely educated . . .

---

1. cf. Also in *Aylwin,* Wilderspin speaking: 'Pre-Raphaelites? The Master rhymes . . . and Burne-Jones actually *reads* the rhymes! However, they are on the right track in art, though neither has the slightest intercourse with the spirit world, not the slightest.'

no one knows the real primal meaning of that pathetic word Man — no one knows the true meaning of Man's position here among the other living creatures of this world, if he has never wanted food. Hunger gives a new seeing to the eyes'. 'I thank God,' he concludes, 'that I once wanted food.'

And again: 'Art became now my religion; success in it my soul's goal. I went to London; I soon began to develop a great power of design . . . For years I worked at this, improving in execution with every design, but still unable to find an opening for a better class of work. What I yearned for was the opportunity to exercise the gift of colour. That I did possess this in a rare degree I knew. At last I got a commission. Oh! the joy of painting that first picture! My progress was now rapid. But I had few purchasers till Providence sent me a good man and great gentleman, my dear friend-----.'[1] 'I never exhibited in the Academy,' he resumes, after a pause. 'I never tried to exhibit; but thanks to the dear friend I have mentioned, I got to know the Master himself [presumably Rossetti]. People came to my poor studio, and my pictures were bought from my easel as fast as I could paint them. I could please my buyers, I could please my dear friend, I could please the Master himself; I could please every person in the world but one — myself. For years I had been struggling with what cripples so many artists — with ignorance — ignorance of the million points of detail which must be understood and mastered before ever the sweetness, the apparent lawlessness and abandonment of Nature can be expressed by Art. But it was now, when I had conquered these, — it was now that I was dissatisfied, and no man living was so miserable as I.' That passage seems to me to come pretty close to the authentic Smetham.

Here, finally, is what seems to be a partial portrait; 'He stood there, the large, full, deep, brown eyes gazing apparently at something over my head a long way off . . . I had noticed that 'Visionary' was stamped upon this man's every feature — that he seemed an inspired baby of forty . . . the sun falling upon his long, brown, curly hair, mixed with grey, which fell from beneath his hat and floated around his collar like a mane.' There is also, in much the same place, a highly significant reference to the 'sedateness' which one would have expected to find (and did *not* find) in Wilderspin.

It is interesting, by the way, to note that in one passage Wilderspin is described by Watts-Dunton as being largely, if not wholly, of Welsh

1 Perhaps Mr. Budgett (see *post.*)

origin, despite his English name. I do not think there is any foundation for this. Nor can I say how just Watts-Dunton's rendering may be in the other passages I have quoted, though I think that, in the absence of better evidence, it cannot be entirely without value.

And here, perhaps, since we are already deep in the Pre-Raphaelite country, it may be proper to touch upon the little that we know of Smetham's relations with the artists of that school — Rossetti and Madox Brown and Frederic Shields. I had myself supposed that the link with Rossetti had come through Ruskin, but Davies conjectures that the two men had met earlier, when Smetham was at Cary's, preparing for the Academy Schools, in 1843. Whether this was so or not, their acquaintance was renewed in 1851 and had ripened into close friendship by 1862, the year in which Smetham took Davies to visit Rossetti in the famous flat that he then occupied at the top of a tall house near Blackfriars Bridge. There they foregathered in a room hung round with Elizabeth Siddal's pictures, from the windows of which they could look out on to the Thames and the Surrey hills beyond.

After Rossetti moved to Cheyne Walk, Smetham formed the habit of spending each Wednesday painting in his studio, while the evenings were passed with some one or other of Rossetti's set. It was an arrangement that lasted from 1863 to 1868, when Rossetti moved out to Kelmscott. Some small quantity of correspondence is also still extant between the two men, and it was in a letter of November 21, 1865, that Rossetti puts a skilfully diagnostic finger on the crucial difference that existed between them:

'I am afraid you will think no better of me for pronouncing the commonplace verdict that what you lack is simply ambition *i.e.* the feeling of pure rage and self-hatred when any one else does better than you do. This in an ambitious mind leads not to envy in the least, but to self-scrutiny on all sides, and that to something if anything can. You comfort yourself with other things, whereas art must be its own comforter . . .

Many years later, in 1906, Rossetti's brother, William Michael, long after Smetham was in his grave, summed up that last sentence in still more forcible terms: 'Painting was his profession and enjoyment; religion was his life . . . Pondering his narrow fortunes, Bible in hand, and brooding over the frequent Old Testament promises that Jehovah would amply provide for the worldly well-being of the devout, [Smetham] came to the conclusion that he must too truly be a reprobate, exposed to the divine displeasure in this world and the next. He totally broke down under this strain upon his mind and feelings.' Strong words, but not necessarily therefore untrue.[1]

As for the rest of the Rossetti circle, little can now be recovered of Smetham's relations with Shields and that is a pity, since, in his way, Shields was very nearly as odd a character as was Smetham. Nor do we know much about his friendship with Madox Brown, save that, as most others did, he found Brown's society wholly delightful; 'cram-full of all that makes my mental life sweet and pleasant. A visit to him is like a walk on a breezy shore with the scent of cockles, and mussels, and sea-weed.'

(v)

Of the fruits of these eight-and-sixty years of struggle and aspiration and defeat what now are left? There are a couple of small books published posthumously in the 'nineties, the so called *Literary Works* and the volume of *Letters* which has already been partially described. There are also the names of a fair number of paintings, some of which are still to be seen, though many have vanished, at least for the time being.

To turn first to the books, the *Literary Works* consists of four essays (long book-reviews, in fact), three of which were originally published in the *London Quarterly Review*: 'Sir Joshua Reynolds'[2] (Jan. 1866); 'Alexander Smith' (Oct. 1868) and, much the most important of all, 'William Blake' (Jan 1869) which, written after the first appearance of Gilchrist's *Life of Blake*, so deeply impressed Rossetti that he reprinted it almost *en bloc* in the second edition of that book. I have already, at the start of this article, recorded Rossetti's conviction that there was a special sort of sympathy between Smetham and Blake and it may therefore be of interest to set down here a few of the further observations that Smetham made concerning his great predecessor, as they are recorded, with less formality than in his essay, in the *Letters.* They were not completely laudatory ones; his verdict on the question

1. An interesting side-light on Smetham's relations with the Pre-Raphaelites is given by a letter of February 8 [1891] now in the Warrington Public Library, from Jane Morris to William Davies, acknowledging the gift of a copy of Smetham's *Letters.* 'I had no idea [she writes] he was so thoughtful a man. I heard stories of him often from Gabriel, but he never led me to believe there was so much real feeling and genuine charm combined with his somewhat eccentric qualities. I should have delighted in his conversation and valued his opinion more than most men's who have a serious reputation.'

2. Though, as is the case with most book-reviews, the majority of the facts in this essay come from the book reviewed, Smetham's final conclusion on Sir Joshua is characteristically his own:'Whatever he could reach by vision and taste he could do, but the gates of imagination were closed and sealed to him.' (*Lit. Wks.* p.91)

whether or not Blake was wholly sane is 'mad but harmless'; yet how greatly to the point is the following: 'Blake is certainly a teaser. He remains in England, where alone he is known, the very best test I know of a man's capacity for seeing the highest essentials of art, the perception of sublimity and beauty when utterly denuded and divorced from externals . . . If a man can see and feel that which makes Blake what he is, he can see and feel anything . . . The right understanding of him becomes a kind of second sight. He was 'intromitted into the spirit world', as Swedenborg said he was, which means simply that he had the ghostly sensibility, the apprehension of what was supernatural, not only in the representation of angels, spirits, demons, but of the spirit that is in man on the earth. His men and women have ghosts inside them, and that's what can be said of not so many.'

The fourth essay is a short appreciation of Gerhard Dow which was first published in the *Art Journal* of 1881; and the volume concludes with a small collection of Smetham's verses, interesting to have in view of his strictures, given earlier, on painters who dared express themselves in this mode. One other essay of his still apparently remains unreprinted; it was published in the *London Quarterly Review* of 1861, and its subject was 'Religious Art in England'.

The *Letters* is a book much less easy to describe than the *Literary Works* because, though it is tight-packed with fine things, it nevertheless possesses a curious formlessness which comes, perhaps, from unskilful editing, or over-editing. It is, in fact, less a collection of true letters than a kind of commonplace book or diary which gives an admirable picture of the great breadth of Smetham's literary and artistic sympathies and his very acute critical sense, his intense dislike, for instance, in the graphic arts for what he calls the 'look-at-that-leg' school of critics, who pick out trifles to disparage and fail utterly to grasp the broad lines of the conception. So far as his judgments upon his fellow-painters are concerned, it is noteworthy that he is often at odds with the taste of his time and lavishes praise upon such out-of-the-way people as Danby and Dadd, whose work is now much more highly regarded than it was in their own day. He even contrives to make mention of that quite forgotten genius, David Scott, whom he roundly describes as an immensely greater man than Millais; and when he finds some of his pictures in a dark corner of William Bell Scott's studio, unnoticed and unknown, he breaks out into a prophecy that might well apply to his own works: 'The gradual broadenings of Biography and History,' he says, 'may yet fetch them out to take their place.' Stothard, Crome,

Turner, Constable, Linnell, Fred Walker: he has something to the point to say of them all, and something that is quite his own. And moreover, save for a fleeting jibe or two in such terms as 'a mere David Roberts or view-taker', his comments are always directed towards the merits not the demerits of the man he is discussing. When Millet died, he wrote: 'What is fame? How obtained? This man is unknown, yet well known. Unknown to the populace, well known to the man of culture. Yet he lived half his life in a village in France, going among the hamlets of France as solitary as a coot; in barns, in wide waste-fields, among potato-heaps, on portentous evenings when the labourer hove up against the bars of fading horizon light and looked solemn at him.'

He was, as this and hundreds of other equally impressive passages show, a born writer with a gift of going straight to the root of the matter. Witness his remark elsewhere, concerning himself: 'I've been poking about Zion for near thirty years, a poor limping tramp, let in and tolerated as yet, and I can't but aver that I see nothing but strength and beauty in Zion; green pastures, still water, strong towers, vines and olives and shady fig-trees, quiet resting-places, springs that bubble more and more brightly and spring up like Jacob's well.' Traherne and his orient and immortal wheat comes at once to mind: here are men of the same order — Traherne at Teddington, Smetham at Stoke Newington; though Smetham's century was the grubbier.

Though always, as the *Letters* abundantly reveal, a man in love with life, with nature, with art, there are other aspects of his complex character to be reckoned with. For all his mysticism, Smetham was an eccentric, too, and parts of his book are couched in the veritable accents of Wilderspin. He can also, in his own playful way, at times be very funny, as when, on the occasion of his forty-first birthday, someone presents him with a pair of gloves, and he recalls how, for the past eight weeks, he has only possessed a solitary one, with which he 'took in' his public. 'The public [he writes] has been living under the delusion that I have had a whole pair of gloves, whereas, by a dazzling series of manoeuvres with one, they have lived in a hollow cheat. I shall now go on a different tack, making such a display as to convey somehow the impression that I have four hands instead of two (all with gloves on), and that I have a brand new pair on every morning. This will lead to the supposition that I must be very well off indeed; which will lead people to buy my pictures.'

There is, it is true, a darker side to his personality which is manifested when, as he sometimes does, he ventures upon theological speculation. It was natural for him to do so, for he had, after all, been for many years a Methodist class-leader; and if from time to time his general liveliness should have become bogged down in the kind of meditation suited to one who had conscientiously pursued this role, it was only in character. Luckily, however, it does not happen often, or for long; the natural zest and curiosity of his disposition soon tends to reassert itself, and he is off upon some new enthusiasm. He was, for one thing, a tremendous reader, both of poetry and of fiction, so that his book is full of the most sagacious and individual comments on his great contemporaries — on Tennyson and Rossetti, on Dickens, on Thackeray, on George Eliot and D'Israeli, on, particularly, the Brontës who were his especial favourites. His criticism of *Wuthering Heights*, though much too long to give here, is one of the best things in the *Letters*, and it was written, moreover, long before it was the fashionable thing to think highly of Emily Brontë.

In short, the real virtue of this little book comes from the extraordinary zest with which Smetham handles whatever he chooses to write about, whether it be natural scenery, or painting, or literature. No-one was ever more a praiser; there is none of the 'Look-at-that-leg' about *his* criticism. Nor does he neglect the human scene; one of the pinnacles of the book is the marvellous account that he gives of his first visit to the Ruskin home, with his hilarious descriptions of old Mr. and Mrs. Ruskin; but he can do simpler things just as well. Witness his account of a walk along the Lower Road, Islington, where he encounters, first, a grocer 'getting bald, looking so respectable. . . that I stood and stared at him. He thought I was admiring his shop and should become a customer.' He is succeeded by a man in a window, twisting wire into toasting-forks — 'honest nice man, liked that man; scrubby looking, but I honoured him . . . honoured him more than the respectable grocer.' It is pure Gissing; and Gissing before his time.

And so on. It is, alas, not possible in the space here available to give more than a taste of the essential manner of this wonderful, if on occasions maddening, volume. One can only recommend it, with the uneasy knowledge that it has now for years been out of print and is not easy to come by. A pity, this, for I suppose it is true to say that, if Smetham's name is at present remembered, it is largely because of the portrait he has drawn of himself in these *Letters*. William Davies who compiled the book[1] was able to do for Smetham what he had never

1. Much of the material that Davies used is now in the Library of Westfield College, University of London.

managed to do for himself, for all the years of heart-breaking effort that had gone to the making of those marvellous Knowledge Books. Yet I suppose it is only fair to add that those books were created far less to catch the eye of posterity than because of Smetham's need to bear witness; to bear witness to his determination that no scrap from the banquet of his life should be lost.

(vi)

Unless and until these Knowledge Books become available for inspection, Smetham's only other claim to recognition as a graphic artist must rest upon such of his paintings as have survived, and these appear to be few. So few that I have decided to make this section very largely a bare catalogue of such of them as I have been able to name. Though in many cases we do not know the size of them, I think it may be taken for granted that they were usually small, Smetham's preference tending always towards the miniature, as may be seen, for example, in his essay praising the work of Gerhard Dow. It may also, I think, even more be taken for granted that the great bulk of the larger and later pictures, and particularly the scriptural ones, had their origin in some particularly happy sketch that was first set down in one or other of the books that subserved the Monumentalist doctrine. It should perhaps also be added that most of the pictures that I have seen have been signed, though sometimes only with initials; and that, of all the works hereafter listed, only two — *Caedmon* and *The Hymn of the Last Supper* — had anything like a substantial price attached to them.

Here, then, is the catalogue. It will be seen that many of the pictures here listed can no longer be located. It has been compiled in the hope that some of these may be discovered because of it, and that must be my apology for it, and for its fragmentary condition: —

Pictures included in the Printed Catalogues of the Liverpool Academy at Old Post-Office Place, Church Street, Liverpool

1848 Eight Pictures: The Reverie 12" x 12"; Portrait of a Gentleman; The Brookside 10" x 12" (painted 1843); Portrait of a Man of the Order of Mercy; Portrait of a Lady; Portrait of John Gray Esq. of Newport, Lincoln; Portrait of Mrs. Gray; Portrait of a Gentleman (no prices given).

1856 Eight Pictures: Dream of the Sea Mist, 12" x 20" oval top, 30 gns.; Mont Blanc and the Valley of Chamounix, 10 gns. (? see the Stone Gallery catalogue, winter 1968, second item); Happy Sleep, 10 gns.; Naboth in his Vineyard, 30 gns. (now in the Tate Gallery as Naboth's Vineyard, oil on panel, 8¾" x 6¾"); Lake of the Four Cantons, 10 gns.; The Field Flower, 15 gns.; The Faithful Messenger, 6" x 8", 15 gns.; Very Interesting, 16" x 12", 25 gns.

1857 Two Pictures: The Chestnut Blossom, £30; Miranda, 30" x 23", £30.

1858 Two Pictures: The Nurse, 10 gns.; Sketch on the Shore, 10 gns.

1859 Eight Pictures: Quiet Fields, 10 gns. (probably Quiet Meadows, Eastbourne, oils, 6" x 10", painted 1854 on his honeymoon, collection Denis Smetham); The Bower, 15 gns.; Ullswater, £21; Flight of a Youth, 4 gns.; Spell-Bound, £25; Death of Earl Siward, 3 gns. (see also 'other dated pictures' under 1861); Flight of Porphyro and Madeline, 3 gns. (now in the Tate Gallery as The Eve of St. Agnes, pen and ink drawings touched with colour, 3¼" x 4", and dated 1858); Initiation of the Emperor Julian, 4 gns.

1862 Two Pictures: Moses and Olivia, probably 4" x 10" and also known as Olivia and the Squire, 10 gns.; Caedmon Playing before Hilda, Abbess of Whitby, 30" x 48", £185 (painted 1861) (see also 'other dated pictures' for 1860).

Note: The 1863 catalogue has not been preserved; there is nothing for 1864 and subsequent years.

Pictures Exhibited at the Royal Academy

1851   The Flageolet, 20" x 14" (painted 1849); Portrait of a Child; Portrait.

1852   Christ at Emmaus, oil on panel, 20" x 15¾" (painted 1849): exhibited at the Royal Academy, 'Victorian and Edwardian Decorative Art — the Handley-Read Collection', March-April, 1972; The Bird-Catchers, 10" x 12" (painted 1849).

1853   A portrait. (Probably of Mrs. Rogers).

1854   Portrait of Mrs Sugden; Portrait of William Davies. (Mrs. Sugden was the wife of the head of the Westminster Normal College).

1855   Counting the Cost. (Luke XIV, 28).

1856   Portrait of James Hoby, for the Wesleyan Education Committee.

1857   The Chestnut Blossom. (See also Liverpool, 1857).

1858   The Nurse (see also Liverpool, 1858); Anna Kull *or* Kuhl, oil 24" x 33" (A portrait of a well-known 'cellist, now in the collection of Mrs. Muriel Smetham, Bloemfontein, South Africa).

1859   A Study; A Portrait.

1862   Mr. Robert Levett and Dr. Johnson visiting a poor family, oil 8" x 8" (based on the etching of 1861).

1863   The Moorland Edge, 24" x 36" (based on the etching).

1869   The Hymn of the Last Supper, oil 24" x 36" (described by G. F. Watts as 'a great picture though it is a small one'; sold for 300 gns. to J.S. Budgett of Stoke Park, the son of the great west-country provision-merchant, Samuel Budgett (1794-1851). A smaller study for the picture, 10" x 15" was sold in 1873 to Lord Mount-Temple for 120 gns.).

Other Dated Pictures in Approximate Chronological Order

1842   The Young Appollo. (Admission drawing for the Academy School, *Letters*, p.14).

1844   Self-portrait, 'Thoughts too deep for tears', oil on panel, $7\frac{7}{8}$" x $5\frac{3}{4}$". Ashmolean Museum, presented by S. W. Hutton, the artist's son-in-law. Reproduced Grigson, *Cornhill*, Autumn, 1948.

c.1845 Self-portrait, chalk and wash, $5\frac{7}{8}$" x $4\frac{7}{8}$". National Portrait Gallery; until 1966 in the possession of the Smetham family.

1851   Moorland Scene, oil, 14" x 6". Collection Basil Smetham.

1852   Othello, oil, 22" x 16". Collection Denis Smetham.

1853   The Lady of Shalott, 20" x 32" (rejected by the Academy, *Letters* p.55). Collection Mrs Janet Smetham, South Africa. The lady is lying on a couch holding a mirror in which Lancelot is reflected.

1853   Self-portrait, oil, oval 8" x 6" (reproduced as frontispiece to the *Letters* and referred to by John Piper on our first page). Sold by Agnew's, formerly in the possession of the Smetham family.

1853-65 'If the blind lead the blind', ink and wash, 4¾" x 4½". Private Collection.

1855   Mother and Baby, oil, 27" x 33", a portrait of Sarah Smetham and her eldest son. Collection Denis Smetham.

1859   The Enchanted Princess *or* The Sleeping Beauty, oil. ('In which the stiff figure of a girl lies across the picture on a red couch before an arcade of flame-green which pierces deeply to the background.' Grigson, *op. cit.* Owned at one time by Messrs. Shepherd Bros. and sold in 1903 to Mr Maitland for £15).

1860   Caedmon Singing, oil, 14" x 12". Collection Denis Smetham. (Presumably a sketch for the picture exhibited at Liverpool in 1862).

c.1860 The Story of Tobias (Apocrypha), oil on panel in eight small scenes, four circular panels $3\frac{1}{8}''$ diameter and four panels $3\frac{1}{8}'' \times 3\frac{1}{8}''$. Exhibited at the Royal Academy, 'Victorian and Edwardian Decorative Art — the Handley-Read Collection', March-April 1972.

1861 Design for a woodcut: the frontispiece to *Snow-bound in Cleeberrie Grange* by G. E. Roberts. British Museum Print Room.

1861 The Death of Earl Siward, oil, 20" x 14". Collection Denis Smetham. Reproduced Grigson *op. cit.* (See also Liverpool Academy 1859, sixth item, and the etching of 1861).

1863 The Maori Chiefs, oil, 34" x 72". Now in the Hocken Library, University of Otago, Dunedin, New Zealand.

1864 The Lobster Pot Mender, oil on panel, 4½" x 6¼". Collection Geoffrey Grigson. Reproduced Maas, *Victorian Painters*.

1864 Ditto, water colour 19" x 7½". Collection Denis Smetham.

1864 Ditto, water colour 18" x 24". Collection Denis Smetham.

1864 Prospero and Miranda, water colour, 10" x 14". Collection Denis Smetham. (See also 'after 1871' for oil version of the same, or similar, subject).

1864 Hugh Miller, water colour, 12" x 24". Collection Denis Smetham. (See also No. 4 of the etchings, *Studies from a Sketch Book*).

1864(?) A Friar riding up hill, accompanied by two dogs, oil on panel, 8½" x 4". Collection Mrs. Peppiatt.

1864 'Men will praise thee, when thou doest well to thyself.' (Ps. XLIX, 18). Oil on panel, 4½" x 7¼". Maas Gallery catalogue, P7528.

1864 Poultry, doves and a peacock in a barn, oil on panel, 4" x 5". (From the collection of D. G. Rossetti). Maas Gallery catalogue, P6800.

1865-72 'Who Touched Me?', oil, 10" x 12". Collection Denis Smetham.

1866 The Lute Player, oil on canvas, 19" x 15¼" (from the collection of James Englebert Vanner). Partly painted by D. G. Rossetti. Maas Gallery catalogue P7719. There are also possibly other versions of this picture, called 'Irene' or 'The Mandoline'; but they are of different size and date.

1866 Going to the Temple, 10" x 13". Collection Denis Smetham (See next item).

1867   Going to the Temple, oil on panel, 12" x 16". Maas Gallery catalogue, P5310.

1867   Fishermen Returning, oil, 4½" x 13½". Sold at Christie's, June 15, 1973, to Gibbs for 1,000 gns. Reproduced in Christie's catalogue of that date. (There may also be another version size 8" x 16").

1867   Seagulls, oil on panel, 4" x 12". Collection Mrs. Virginia Surtees. Reproduced Maas, *Victorian Painters.*

1867   Pagan Rites, oil on panel, 12" x 16¼". Collection: Allan Hogg.

1868   A 10" study sold to Agnew (*Letters*, p.212). Probably, 'Ye hypocrites', Luke XII, 56, oil, 6" x 10".

1868   Winter Shore, oil, 6" x 14". Collection Denis Smetham.

1868-69 Bognor, Shore Scene, water colour, $8\frac{3}{16}$" x $11\frac{11}{16}$". Ashmolean Museum, presented by S. W. Hutton, the artist's son-in-law. (Smetham was at Bognor in 1868 and 1869).

1868-69 The Shadow of the Cross; possibly never finished. (*Letters* p.222, 225).

1869   That Bedesman Old, oil, 12" x 18" Collection Denis Smetham. Exhibited at Birmingham City Museum and Art Gallery: 'The Pre-Raphaelite Brotherhood,' 1947 and at the Whitechapel Art Gallery: 'The Pre-Raphaelites', 1948.

1869   The Abbot's Walk, oil, 13" x 18". Collection Denis Smetham.

1870   Orpheus looking after Eurydice, oil, 12" x 14". Collection Denis Smetham.

1870   The Casket, oil, 34" x 24". Collection Denis Smetham.

1870   Lady Macbeth, oil, 14" x 20". Collection Denis Smetham.

1870   The Women of the Crucifixion, crayon, 46" x 34" Collection Denis Smetham. (A full size study for the painting of 1871).

1871   Evening, Deer, oil, 8" x 20". Collection Denis Smetham.

1871   The Women of the Crucifixion, oil, 46" x 34" (*Letters*, p.27, see p.24 *ante*). Rejected by the Academy, the picture was sold to J. S. Budgett for 350 gns.

1871   Hesper, oil, 34" x 48" (*Letters*, p.27). Rejected by the Academy, sold to J. S. Budgett for 250 gns.

1871   Driving Sheep, oil on panel, $4\frac{7}{8}$" x $11\frac{7}{8}$". Ashmolean Museum, presented by S. W. Hutton, the artist's son-in-law. (Also entitled 'Twilight' on contemporary label on back of the frame).

After
1871   The Dream of Pilate's Wife, oil, 30" x 38". (*Letters*, p.28). Rejected by the Academy, sold to J. F. Hall of Sharcombe, near

Wells, Somerset, for 150 gns. This picture was seen in Smetham's studio by the American artist, Elihu Vedder, who wrote that 'the blood-red counterpane seemed like a sea of blood creeping up towards her breasts, threatening to overwhelm her as she lay under the spell of some nightmare.'

After
1871   Prospero and Miranda, oil (*Letters,* p. 27). Rejected by the Academy. (See also water colour of 1864).

1872   The Farmer's Gun, oil, 8" x 14". Collection Denis Smetham.

1872   Geese: study, oil, 14" x 18". Collection Denis Smetham.

1873   A picture depicting a dragon in a fen 'of which Rossetti had a great opinion', once the property of Watts-Dunton (*Aylwin,* Appendix II). It is also referred to in *Letters* p.326 under 1873: 'I found a wonderful image in *Coriolanus* . . . and have begun it on a twelve-inch panel: 'Like to a lonely dragon that his fen/Makes fear'd and talk'd of more than seen.' (Act IV, sc. i, 32-33). Oil, 4" x 10". Rossetti owned the picture before Watts-Dunton.

1874   Groynes on the Beach, Bognor, water colour, 5" x 12". Collection Denis Smetham.

1874   Rose of Dawn, oil, 9" x 4". Collection Denis Smetham. (See catalogue of the Stone Gallery, Newcastle-upon-Tyne, Winter, 1968, for the final version of this picture).

1874   Druid Stone, Avon Valley, water colour, 8" x 12". Collection Denis Smetham.

1874   Landscape, Valley of the Avon, water colour, 5" x 7". Collection Denis Smetham.

1875   Call of the Prophet Amos, oil, 10" x 24". Collection Denis Smetham.

1876   Piping Down the Valley[s], water colour, 8" x 12". Collection Denis Smetham.

1876   Piping Down the Valley[s], water colour, 6" x 4". Collection Denis Smetham.

1876   Piping Down the Valley[s], water colour, 2½" x 7". Collection Sir Geoffrey Keynes.

1877   'The Nymphs in Twilight Shade' (Milton's 'Ode on the Morning of Christ's Nativity'), drawing, $11\frac{3}{4}$" x $18\frac{7}{8}$". Nottingham Museum and Art Gallery. (Described as 'figures in an extensive landscape'; painted on a substratum of Chinese white with a glass medium).

1877 'Looking on the Happy Autumn Fields', water colour, 3½" x 6". Collection Sir Geoffrey Keynes.

1877 Going Home. (*Letters*, p.379: 'Levelling in cobalt and rose madder clouds in Going Home'). Probably the water colour 12" x 18" sold to Mr. Fishwick Stead for 50 gns.

1877(?) Study for 'Going Home', pencil heightened with white, 7" x 4¾". Maas Gallery catalogue, W7144.

1877 Saturn and Vesta. (*Letters*, p.380: 'Smoothing the ravendown of darkness, till it smiled in 'Saturn and Vesta', infusing more gold into the dim flesh tints by infinitely small touches.')

1877 Sixty small sketches. (*Letters*, p. 383: 'I got sixty small sketches and other memoranda during my boatings and goings among the islands on the coast of Scotland.')

Other Undated Pictures

Landscape, water colour, 3¾″ x 5½″. Victoria and Albert Museum.

Paris and Œnone, brush drawing in brown touched with white. British Museum Print Room.

Figure standing by a Tree, water colour, $4\frac{5}{8}$″ x $4\frac{7}{8}$″. Ashmolean Museum, presented by Mr. Denis Smetham. (A similar composition in oil belonged to the artist's son-in-law, S. W. Hutton).

Beachy Head, oil on board, $6\frac{7}{8}$″ x 10″. Ashmolean Museum, presented by Mr. Denis Smetham.

Shepherd and Shepherdess with a flock; water and body colour with outlining in ink, 5¼″ x 13¾″. Ashmolean Museum, presented by Mr. Denis Smetham.

Sheet of studies of four women, sewing, resting etc. also a baby's head, and hand holding a spear (?), pencil and water colour, 9¾″ x 6¾″. Ashmolean Museum, presented by the artist's son-in-law, S. W..Hutton.

Christ in the Garden of Gethsemane, pen, indian ink and water colour, $5\frac{1}{8}$″ x $7\frac{15}{16}$″. Fitzwilliam Museum.

Hereward the Wake, water colour, $7\frac{7}{16}$″ x $4\frac{1}{2}$″ sheet size, the subject is small. City Museum and Art Gallery, Birmingham. (Smetham's friend, Charles Mansford, was the model for Hereward and, for the girl, Miss Mansford, later Lady Newsholme, wife of the donor).

Jacob at Bethel, oil on panel, $4\frac{3}{8}$″ x $11\frac{7}{8}$″. City Museum and Art Gallery, Birmingham, donor the same as preceding.

The Many Wintered Crow, oil on panel, $5\frac{1}{2}$″ x $7\frac{5}{8}$″. City Museum and Art Gallery, Birmingham, donor as last. (Inscribed by the artist: 'The many winter'd crow that leads the clanging rookery home': Tennyson,

'Locksley Hall', 1. 68. Described by Mr John Woodward as 'a superb small picture, very dark and luminous.')

Imogen and the Shepherds, oil on canvas, 10" x 24¼". City Museum and Art Gallery, Birmingham. (Cymbeline, Act IV, sc. ii).

[?] 'Who is this that cometh from Edom?', water colour, 4" 5¾". Collection Mrs. Imogen Dennis.

Portrait of Revd. James Smetham (1792-1847), the father of the artist, oil, 24" x 29". Collection Denis Smetham.

Portrait of Mrs. Goble, mother-in-law of the artist, oil, 30" x 24½". Collection Denis Smetham.

Medieval Subject: Knight kneeling, water colour, 11" x 10". Collection Denis Smetham. (Exhibited at the Whitechapel Art Gallery: 'The Pre-Raphaelites', 1948).

Feeding of the Five Thousand, water colour, 4¾" x 6". Collection Denis Smetham. (Exhibited at Whitechapel, as last item).

An Elizabethan House, water colour, 8" x 6". Collection Denis Smetham.

Season of Mists and Mellow Fruitfulness, water colour, 5¾" x 3¾". Collection Denis Smetham.

Reaper in Cornfield (landscape) oil, 11½" x 7½". Collection Denis Smetham.

Dante in Italy (?). Probably 'Dante in Vallombrosa', oil, 8" x 6". Collection Denis Smetham.

Girl holding Flower, oil, 15" x 10". Collection Denis Smetham.

Female Head, water colour, 3½" x 4". Collection Denis Smetham.

Crow with Carrion, water colour, 6½" x 3". Collection Denis Smetham.

Land- and sea-scape, water colour, 6½" x 4". Collection Denis Smetham.

Old Barn, Ongar, water colour, 3½" x 4½". Collection Denis Smetham.

Organ Grinder on Seashore, water colour, 7½" x 4½". Collection Denis Smetham.

Women reading with sea in background, water colour, 4" x 6½". Collection Denis Smetham.

Knight on horseback galloping with castle in the background, water colour, 7" x 5". Collection Denis Smetham.

Rural landscape with women walking in the foreground, water colour, 7½" x 5". Collection Denis Smetham.

Five figures of men and women seated in a shelter on a seaside promenade, water colour, 9" x 5". Collection Denis Smetham.

Mythical figure in the grip of (?) an octopus, water colour, 6" x 3¾". Collection Denis Smetham.

Groyne on sand-dunes, water colour, 9¾" x 7". Collection Denis Smetham.

Seascape with cliffs and fish on rock in the foreground, water colour, 6¾" x 4". Collection Denis Smetham.

Also *five* sketches, framed, from the sketch-books.

Flight of Apollo, oil, 5" x 7". Collection Basil Smetham. (Almost certainly painted in 1875, based on Milton's 'Hymn on the Morning of Christ's Nativity'; xix).

Women at the Sepulchre, oil, 14" x 6". Collection Basil Smetham. (A water colour possibly related to this picture but simply entitled 'Sepulchre', size 11¾" x $7\frac{1}{8}$" was sold at Christie's, June 12, 1973 to Clarke for 380 gns.).

A Young Lady in Exotic Costume. Sold at Sotheby's June 10, 1970 for £900. (*Dictionary of Victorian Painters*, by Christopher Wood, 1971).

Eventide (a single figure at the edge of a wooded pool), water colour, 4" x 8". Sold at Christie's, March 13, 1973 for £2310. (*The Times* sale-room correspondent).

The Lily Lake, water colour heightened with white, $3\frac{1}{8}$" x $8\frac{1}{8}$" (Collection Besterman 1969, No. 69. Maas Gallery catalogue, W8074). Perhaps related to etching No. 12: The Water Lily.

'He alone on the land', oil on board, 4" x 5½", inscribed No. 5. (Maas Gallery catalogue, P 8026). Perhaps related to etching No. 4: 'Hugh Miller watching for his Father's Vessel'.

Portrait study of Patrick Mathews, pen and ink, $7\frac{3}{8}$" x $5\frac{3}{4}$", inscribed. Maas Gallery catalogue, W7782.

Eminent Connoisseurs, pen and ink, 6" x 4". Maas Gallery catalogue, W6399.

Allegorical Subject, oil on board, 5" x 9". Maas Gallery catalogue, Autumn 1972, W8045.

Unfinished sketch of 'a mad-looking Ruskin, with eyes like an insect's inverted, each at the end of a long tunnel'. (Information from Mr. Geoffrey Grigson).

An illustration to Milton's Sonnet to Mr. Lawrence, once the property of William Davies (*Letters*, p.25). This picture, or a water colour replica of it, 14" x 6", is now in the collection of Basil Smetham.

A water colour representing 'a mysterious traveller draped in a shawl or plaid hasting over a heath, backed by a storm-cloud. Behind him in the distance an ass is seen grazing, whilst just in front of him is a milestone marked with vague figures.' Probably symbolic of Smetham's own career. (*Letters*, p.25). This picture, 'The Belated Traveller', based on a sketch of 1851, was painted in 1871 for William Davies, size 2" x 5".

Pictures Undated, and for the Most Part Untitled in the Collection of Mrs. Muriel Smetham, Bloemfontein, South Africa.

Small figure of a woman with arms outspread, by water, in what seems to be a cave. Oil, 20½″ x 8″. (This might be the 'Ophelia' painted in 1874).

Fisherman and woman with lobster-pots on a beach with a breakwater and the sea in the background. Oil, 20½″ x 11″. (Very possibly a Bognor shore-scene, painted about 1868).

Mariana: 'She drew her casement-curtain by,/And glanced athwart the glooming flats' (Tennyson). Oil, 8½″ x 7″. (Perhaps painted about 1865).

Woman with tambourine, man with a flute, oil, 6″ x 6″.

Edge of a lake with figure in right hand lower corner and standing monoliths, oil, 18″ x 9″. (Perhaps related to 'Druid Stone, Avon Valley', 1874 in collection of Denis Smetham).

Man in foreground, sunset on horizon over the sea, oil, 18″ x 9″.

Saul 'hiding among the stuff'. (1 Samuel, x, 22). Oil, 6″ x 6″.

Small figures of horsemen in red tunics riding across a desert, oil, 11¾″ x 4″.

The Vision of Sin: 'I had a vision when the night was late:/A youth came riding toward a palace-gate./He rode a horse with wings, that would have flown,/But that his heavy rider kept him down./And from the palace came a child of sin,/And took him by the curls, and led him in.' (Tennyson). Oil, 7½″ x 4¾″. (Painted in 1872).

Rose of Dawn: '. . . I heard a voice upon the slope,/Cry to the summit, "Is there any hope?" . . . And on the glimmering limit far withdrawn/God made Himself an awful rose of dawn.' (Tennyson, "The Vision of Sin".) Oil, 5″ x 9″. (No doubt an oil sketch or a small replica of the painting hereafter included from the Stone Gallery catalogue, executed in 1874).

'A large pavilion like a mountain peak/Sundered the glooming [or gloaming] crimson on the marge.' Oil, 14" x 6½".

Miranda (head and shoulders), oil, 21" x 25". (Two Mirandas, differing in size from this one, were painted in 1856).

A skeleton on a skeleton horse and an old man on a white horse, apparently galloping through the air; (?) Death and Time. Pen and ink, 4½" x 6½".

Note: There are also other pictures in South Africa, in the collection of Mrs. Janet Smetham, details of which (except for the 1853 'Lady of Shalott') are not at present available. Mrs. Matthews, her daughter, however, has the following in her possession:

The Ford; a knight in armour crossing a ford on horseback, oil, 3¾" x 2¾".

Two men on a sand dune looking out to sea with a telescope, oil, 19½" x 7¾".

The Husbandman and the Stork (from Aesop's *Fables*), showing a man catching a stork with two dead birds beside him, and two women in a cornfield, 22" x 13".

Items from the Catalogues of the
Stone Gallery, Newcastle-Upon-Tyne

Winter 1968

'The plague is begun.' Ink and wash, 2¾" x 3½", 1859. (From the Smetham family).

First sight of Mont Blanc, water colour, 3¼" x 6¼". (From the Smetham family. See also a similar item in the Liverpool Academy catalogue for 1856).

Young man reclining in a field, pencil, 2¾" x 5¾" (From the Smetham family).

An old lady with a candlestick, pencil, 5" diameter. (From the Smetham family).

Mrs. Hindley, sister of the Revd. James Smetham and the painter's aunt, pencil and wash, 5¾" x 4½". (From the Smetham family).

Street scene with hurdy-gurdy man, water colour, 4½" x 7¾". Illustrated. (From the Smetham family).

The Rose of Dawn, oil on canvas, 14" x 24", incorporating a self-portrait. Illustrated both here and in *Summer, 1971.* (The picture is mentioned, obliquely, in *Letters*, p.352, under 1874: 'I am glad to have been gradually forced down from Roses of Dawn to the Foxglove and Rabbit dingles and dells.' After Smetham's collapse in 1877, Rossetti and Frederic Shields mounted in 1878 an exhibition of his pictures in Rossetti's studio; and some of them were sold. After this exhibition Rossetti, persisting in his endeavours to help the family, sold other pictures to various people and in July, 1879, sent twelve Smetham paintings to Edmund Bates, the Leeds art dealer. The 'Rose of Dawn' was, apparently, among these. See also another version of the subject in *Pictures . . . in the Collection of Mrs. Muriel Smetham,* and under 1874 in *Other Dated Pictures*).

Spring 1969

'The country magistrate proposes an attitude for his full length portrait', ink and wash, 6" x 4¾". (The figure on the right is said to be a self-portrait).

Autumn 1969

The Knight's Bride, oil on panel, 12" x 7¼", 1864.

The Vision, oil on canvas, 10" x 23½", 1864. (Also included in *Summer, 1971*, where it is illustrated).

Mary Magdalene, oil on panel, 12" x 7¼", 1868.

Summer 1971

The Ploughman, oil on canvas, 9½" x 23½".

This list, with all its manifold imperfections, includes about one hundred and eighty pictures (excluding the sixty Scottish sketches and the at present unclassified items in the collection of Mrs. Janet Smetham), of which some sixty-eight oils and sixty-three water colours or drawings, most of them small and many of them late, can be located in public and private collections. It is not a selection upon which much of a judgement can be based. Where then, ultimately, does Smetham stand as a painter? William Davies had an interesting theory that he was really an artist of an earlier school — he mentions the name of Wilkie — and that the Pre-Raphaelite afflatus destroyed his natural manner. He was, after all, of an elder generation; Holman Hunt was six years his junior; Rossetti seven; Millais eight; Burne-Jones twelve. It was with men, younger by a generation and more than a generation, with whom, in his later years, he was attempting to keep pace. What he was before Pre-Raphaelitism began, only his early pictures can reveal, and at present these are pitifully few.

It remains a distinct possibility, therefore, that posterity may tend to regard Smetham in much the same way as it does Haydon, as a man who wrote better than he painted. That is for posterity to decide. For myself, I would rather defer judgement until more of his best pictures have come to light and, for the time being, to base my belief in his essential stature as an artist on those astonishing illustrated volumes which, in my view, possess all the qualities of poetic and imaginative genius that Ruskin and Rossetti thought they saw in him. Upon these, and upon that triumphant little masterpiece, his *Letters*, rests most of his present claim to remembrance. Yet we ought not to forget, too, that, in his own odd and entirely individual way, he was unique; he

[53]

belonged to no school and founded none; he was the first, last, and only Monumentalist. It is hard to believe that those dedicated years of 'poking about Zion' with his microscopic eye have gone for nothing.

Works Consulted

Letters of James Smetham, ed. Sarah Smetham and William Davies. 1891.

Literary Works of James Smetham, ed. William Davies. 1893.

Aylwin, by Theodore Watts-Dunton. 1898. With appendixes, 1914.

Some Reminiscences, by W. M. Rossetti. 1906.

The Digressions of Elihu Vedder. 1911.

British Romantic Artists, by John Piper. 1942.

James Smetham, by Geoffrey Grigson. *Cornhill Magazine,* 976 (Autumn 1948), pp.332-346.

Catalogues of the Liverpool Academy.

Catalogues of the Stone Gallery, Newcastle-upon-Tyne. Winter 1968; Spring 1969; Autumn 1969; Summer 1971.

Acknowledgements

My grateful thanks are due to the following people who have generously helped me with information and good counsel:

Edward Croft-Murray of the British Museum Print Room; Christopher J. M. Johnstone of the Tate Gallery; Richard Ormond of the National Portrait Gallery; Brian Reade of the Victoria and Albert Museum; John de Wit of the Ashmolean Museum; Duncan Robinson of the Fitzwilliam Museum; John Gilmartin and Harley Preston of the City Museum and Art Gallery, Birmingham; David Phillips of the City of Nottingham Museum and Art Gallery; C. R. Eastwood F.L.A., the Somerset County Librarian. Also to Dr. David Bindman of Westfield College; Mrs. Imogen Dennis; Mr. Geoffrey Grigson; Mr. Jeremy Maas; Dr. D. E. Rhodes; Mr. R. H. Ronson; Mr. Denis J. Smetham; Mrs. Virginia Surtees; and Mr. John Woodward.

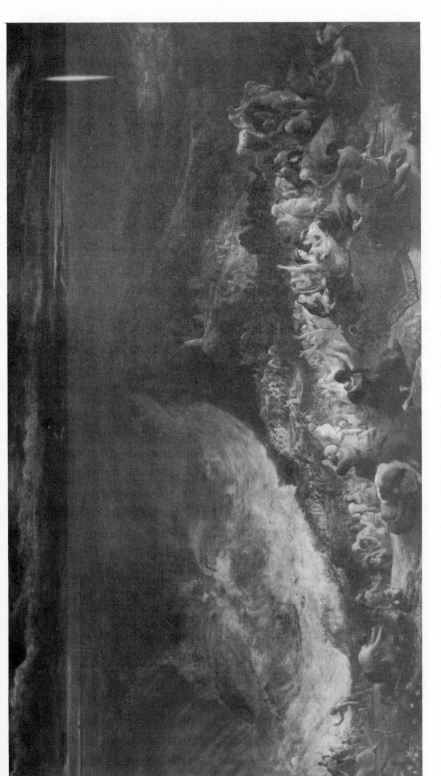

1. Francis Danby: The Delivery of Israel out of Egypt.
Oil on canvas. 58¾ × 94½ inches, 1824-5.
Collection: *Harris Museum and Art Gallery, Preston*

2. Francis Danby: Disappointed Love.
Oil on panel. 24¾ X 32 inches, 1821.
Collection: *Victoria and Albert Museum, London*

3. Francis Danby: St. Vincents Rocks and the Avon Gorge. Pencil and watercolour. 17¾ × 26¾ inches, ca. 1815-8. Collection: *City Art Gallery, Bristol*

4. Francis Danby: The Avon at Clifton.
Watercolour and body colour. 5 × 8 ⅜ inches.

5. Francis Danby: The Frome at Stapleton.
Pencil, watercolour and body colour. 5¾ × 8½ inches
ca. 1821-3. Collection: *City art Gallery, Bristol*

6. Francis Danby: A view of the Avon Gorge.
Oil on panel, 13 X 18 inches, 1822.

7. Francis Danby: The Snuff Mill, Stapleton.
Oil on panel. 8¾ × 12 inches, ca. 1820-21.
Collection: *City Art Gallery, Bristol.*

8. Francis Danby: The Snuff Mill, Stapleton.
Oil on canvas. 15¼ X 24¼ inches, ca. 1820-21.
Collection: *City Art Gallery, Bristol.*

9. Francis Danby: Boy Fishing, Stapleton.
Oil on panel. 5 X 7¼ inches, ca. 1820-21.
Collection: *City Art Gallery, Bristol.*

10. Francis Danby: A Scene in Leigh Woods.
Oil on panel. 13 × 19¾ inches, 1822.

11. Francis Danby: Clifton Rocks from Rownham Fields.
Oil on panel. 15¾ × 20 inches, ca. 1821.
Collection: *City Art Gallery, Bristol.*

12. Francis Danby: Boys Sailing a Little Boat.
Oil on panel. 9¾ × 13¼ inches, ca. 1821.
Collection: City Art Gallery, Bristol.

13. James Arthur O'Connor: The Devil's Glen.
Collection: *National Gallery of Ireland, Dublin.*

14. James Smetham: The Rose of Dawn.
Oil on canvas. 14 × 24 inches.
Collection: *The Stone Gallery.*

15. James Smetham: The Knight's Bride.
Oil on panel. 12 × 7¼ inches, 1864.
Collection: *The Stone Gallery*.

16. James Smetham: Pagan Rites.
Oil on panel. 30 × 41 cms., 1867.
Collection: Allen H.

17. James Smetham: The Vision.
Oil on canvas. 10 × 23½ inches, 1864.
Collection: *The Stone Gallery*

18. James Smetham: Poultry, Doves and Peacocks in a Barn.
Oil on panel. 4 × 5 inches, 1864
Collection: *The Maas Gallery*

19. James Smetham: Mary Magdalene.
Oil on panel. 12 × 7¼ inches, 1868
Collection: *The Stone Gallery*

20. James Smetham: The Lobster Pot Mender.
Oil on panel. 4½ × 6¼ inches, 1864
Collection: *Geoffrey Grigson*

21. James Smetham and D. G. Rossetti: The Lute Player.
Oil on canvas. 19 X 15¼ inches, 1866
Collection: *The Maas Gallery*